CW00606719

# KALEIDOSCOPE

## MONMOUTHSHIRE

Edited by Carl Golder

First published in Great Britain in 1999 by
*POETRY NOW YOUNG WRITERS*
Reumus House,
Coltsfoot Drive, Woodston,
Peterborough, PE2 9 JX
Telephone (01733) 890066

HB ISBN 0 75430 361 6
SB ISBN 0 75430 362 4

# FOREWORD

This year, the Poetry Now Young Writers' Kaleidoscope competition proudly presents the best poetic contributions from over 32,000 up-and-coming writers nationwide.

Successful in continuing our aim of promoting writing and creativity in children, each regional anthology displays the inventive and original writing talents of 11-18 year old poets. Imaginative, thoughtful, often humorous, *Kaleidoscope Monmouthshire* provides a captivating insight into the issues and opinions important to today's young generation.

The task of editing inevitably proved challenging, but was nevertheless enjoyable thanks to the quality of entries received. The thought, effort and hard work put into each poem impressed and inspired us all. We hope you are as pleased as we are with the final result and that you continue to enjoy *Kaleidoscope Monmouthshire* for years to come.

# CONTENTS

Amy Oates                                    21

King Henry VIII School

                Owain Bradley                21
                Tara Hall                    22
                Tom Wood                     22
                Edward Saunders              23
                Kayleigh Moeller             23
                Gareth Staphnill             24
                Stephen Carrett              24
                Jeana Hollands               25
                Alan Jones                   25
                Laura Potts                  26
                Richard Hunt                 26
                Sjabena Sealy                27
                Rhys Thomas Llewellyn        27
                Huw Gullick                  28
                Huw Groucutt                 29
                Racheal Lumpkin              30
                Stuart Phillips              30
                Dani Thomas                  31
                Gemma Trickey                32
                Vicky Batkin                 32
                Jessica Hudson               33
                Adam Phillips                33
                Barley Blyton                34
                Shani Viveash                34
                Samuel Barnor                35
                Jamie Laurent                35
                Neil Harris                  36
                Amy Talbot                   36
                Christopher Wenham           37
                Laura Lewis                  37
                Owen Carr                    38
                Lindsey Perry                38
                Ryan Griffin                 39
                Anna Gray                    40
                Hannah Davies                40

| | |
|---|---:|
| Hannah Brown | 64 |
| Owain Wood | 65 |
| Siân Binns | 66 |
| Cathy Hook | 66 |
| Jennifer Marshall | 67 |
| Steph Turnbull | 68 |
| Charlotte Prosser | 68 |
| Christopher Hill | 69 |
| Verity Turner | 69 |
| Jackie Watkins | 70 |
| Elizabeth Hobson | 70 |
| Martin Adams | 71 |
| Steven Caswell | 72 |
| Laura Terry | 73 |
| Peter Chater | 73 |
| Khwanyo Bu | 74 |
| Alys Cottom | 74 |
| Fiona Bennett | 75 |
| Siân Eve Goldsmith | 76 |
| Sian Robins-Grace | 77 |
| Victoria Bowen | 78 |
| Wayne Llewellyn | 78 |
| Jonathon Ruck | 79 |
| Kieran Shevlin | 80 |
| Gareth Pritchard | 80 |
| Rhiannon Price | 81 |
| Christopher Shephard | 82 |
| Jo Iles | 83 |
| Hayley MacDonald | 84 |
| Lesley Date | 84 |
| Peter Mullen | 85 |
| Rhys Watkins | 85 |
| Catherine Perkins | 86 |
| James Matthews | 86 |
| Holly Bryant | 87 |
| Kevin Carr | 87 |
| Alex Busby | 88 |
| Kate Spooner | 88 |

| | |
|---|---|
| Louise Griffiths | 89 |
| Rachel Page | 90 |
| Jonathan Wolley | 90 |
| Jeni Stokes | 91 |
| Marion Lewis | 92 |
| Charlotte Price | 92 |
| Victoria Griffiths | 93 |
| Donna Assirati | 94 |
| Rhys Harris | 94 |
| Becky Robertson | 95 |
| Natalie Davies | 96 |
| Tristram Hall | 96 |
| Cari Silcox | 97 |
| Billie Prangley | 98 |
| Rhos Williams | 98 |
| Gareth Thomas | 99 |
| Thomas Folan | 99 |
| Robert Bender | 100 |
| Ellie Davis | 101 |
| Mark Edwards | 102 |
| Octavia Younger | 102 |
| Keriane Garton | 103 |
| Imogen Hassall | 104 |
| Simon Jones | 104 |
| Anthony Chaloner | 105 |
| Joe Atkinson | 105 |
| Sam Tutton | 106 |
| Daniel Matthews | 106 |
| Sally Brinkworth | 107 |
| Alex Linney | 107 |
| Lloyd Hughes | 108 |
| Jamie Breakwell | 108 |
| Claire Addis | 109 |
| Catherine Lock | 109 |
| Rebekah Anne Brown | 110 |
| Heather Venfield | 110 |
| Harriet Artes | 111 |
| Sam Morgan | 111 |

*The Poems*

## THANK YOU...

I can't thank you enough
As you chose me, I am chuffed
For the publishing of my poem.
You can't see me but I'm showing
For all the loving I admit
In all my poems I am a bit,
Of everything you see and know.
*Thank you!*
My brain is where it stands,
It's in the middle of my hands.
Because my heart does all the working,
And my poems are all that's showing
*Thank you!*
I hope you're really grateful
For this poem I have written for you,
As it's the only thing which I can give
Which is coming straight from me.
All I really wanted is to say that
I am grateful
For all the effort you have done
To put me in your book.
*Thank you!*
*Thank you very much . . .*

**Vicky Patterson  (14)**

# I STAND ALONE . . .

I stand alone
Nothing around me
Only snow and snow covered trees
No sound,
I begin to walk
Snow crunches under the cautious steps of my feet.
I no longer think I'm alone
I start to run
I hear crunches behind me
I daren't look that way
Sprinting for all I'm worth
Apparently getting nowhere
Trees and brilliant blinding white
No end in sight
I have tripped and fallen
. . .I wake . . .

*Graham Curtis (12)*
*Chepstow Comprehensive School*

# COLOURS

Murky blue skies transform around me,
Above the shimmer of the frosty frozen lake.
The glimmering blue, tinted on the little bluebells.

All these things lie in front of my eyes,
They all have colours, the same colours 'blue'.

Bright blue lights flash constantly as a siren
Goes speeding past.
These are the colours I see
In my eyes.

*Lucy Evans (11)*
*Chepstow Comprehensive School*

# DREAMS!

Dreams are relaxing, peaceful, silent
Like heaven
Like clouds
Magical
Let your thoughts and imagination run wild
You can be anything
Anyone
Do anything
You can do what you want
In your dreams
You can speak to people
Touch other people.
Go with other people
Whatever you want
You can listen to songs
Look at pictures
Anything - anything you want
*You can do . . . in your dreams!*

***Kevin Abell  (12)***
***Chepstow Comprehensive School***


# A DREAM OF CHRISTMAS EVE

It is snowing in my dream
Each snowflake is like a fairy floating to the ground.
They float into my eyes, making me blink.
When I open my eyes again I see a sled being pulled
along by reindeers.
Heading over the moon
Then it disappears, till next year
And I wake up . . .

***Angela Whiteside  (12)***
***Chepstow Comprehensive School***

# THOSE FACES

I can see faces,
Familiar faces,
Just watching,
Staring.
They are there for something,
A purpose
Like my destiny,
Providence.
I wish they would go
To another place.
I'm running,
Fleeing,
But they are still there.
I wake . . .
*And see that painting!*

**Samuel Thomas (12)**
**Chepstow Comprehensive School**


# BLUE

Blue is my favourite colour
that most people like.
Blue is for rivers.
They like crashing from side to side.
Blue is for the sky
White clouds like floating by.
Blue is for the sea
that fish love swimming in.
When I look in the woodland
I see a beautiful carpet of bluebells
What a lovely sight
Of blue . . .

**Charlotte Waters (11)**
**Chepstow Comprehensive School**

# THE PREDATOR!

Alarm bells ring
People awake
Gunshots are heard
People screaming
Soldiers lay dead
It wasn't their day
Lights are flashing.

The beast kills!
Unaffected by human restraints
It moves as quick as lightening
Killing with one swipe
It takes no prisoners
It rips limb from limb.

Suddenly there's a bang!
The light is blinding
It takes an age to clear
Bodies are left to decay
But the beast is dead . . .
People shout with joy
Their lives were spared
*The humans had won . . .*

***Tim Cook  (12)***
***Chepstow Comprehensive School***

## THE JUNGLE GOODBYE ...

The jungle - as still as water
The trees as silent as snow
The hunter as rough as a lion
The lion as flat as a rug.

Now the hunter sweating like a river
The gun perched under his arm
The hideaway as covered as a
Christmas tree
The hand shaking like the wind.

The lion as smooth as silk
The roar like an echo
The feet stepping like butter
The spots like charcoal and mud

*Bang! Bang! Bang!*

Uproar in the forest
The animals run like a stream
The lion as quiet as smoke
The birds as noisy as fire

The hunter as proud as can be
But then what have I done
*That could have been me . . . !*

**James Phillips  (12)**
**Chepstow Comprehensive School**

# A GREY DAY

A misty morning cold and bleak
No sunlight shining through;
And sodden hedges freshly webbed
All glistening with dew . . .

A grey thrush sings a song somewhere
In some murky tree;
All other things are quiet
Sleeping silently . . .

A misty morning once was bleak
But now the sun shines through;
The sky that was a murky grey
Is now a brilliant blue . . .

*Richard Arnatt (11)*
*Chepstow Comprehensive School*


# COLOURS

When a soldier gets shot
Red blood pours everywhere
Yellow daffodils cover the fields
It just makes you sit and stare.

The leaves and the grass
Are a lovely mid-green
The blue sky full of clouds
Can always be seen.

An orange is well
A beautiful orange
And a sauce which is brown and
Has a sparkle like a burnt sausage.

*Thomas Shaw (11)*
*Chepstow Comprehensive School*

## Colour

Blackness slowly drips over the sky.
Redness - a dash of spice.
Silver - it shines and glints just like a knife.
Green - the colour of the trees with a dash
of yellow and brown.
The colours of the world gleam
and glint everywhere.
We let them fade until the sky
is colourless.
No colour in the trees
No colour in the sky
No colour anywhere
*Just plainness . . .*

**Jamie Marmont  (12)**
**Chepstow Comprehensive School**

## Colours

Yellow is a banana - a bright brilliant colour.
Blue is the sea and sky up above.
Orange is a simple orange.
Purple is a plum that tastes so sweet.
Green is the grass and leaves on the trees.
Red is an apple nice and juicy.
Pink are flowers blooming in the summer.
White is the snow in the wintertime.
Gold is on my necklace
And silver is on my shoe . . .

**Alexandra Jones**
**Chepstow Comprehensive School**

## MY COLOUR POEM

Green is for the leaves that hang off a chestnut tree.
It's also for the grass which has many shades,
The green of an apple makes it look so good,
Green are the emeralds that wait for me.

Red is for the wine that comes from France,
For the ripe strawberries we eat in the summer.
Red is a Ferrari on the racing track
And the berries on the holly bush
On a chilly winters day.

Blue are the oceans - so vast and so deep
Blue is the colour of a clear summers sky
Blue can be majestic for Kings and Queens,
But blue is my favourite colour . . .

*Gareth Modget  (11)*
*Chepstow Comprehensive School*


## KALEIDOSCOPE

Yellow - sparkling sun
The silky thick sand
Bright yellow daffodils
Yellow as beautiful as a lemon.
Autumn leaves dropping on the ground
And as tasty as ice cream.

Red as the royal carpet
As red as a rose.
Redder than rosy cheeks
And as thick as blood . . .

*Francesca Kelley  (11)*
*Chepstow Comprehensive School*

# KALEIDOSCOPE

Spinning spinning
Around they go
Never stop spinning
Never go slow . . .

The magical colour
The clicking sound
The blue getting duller
As you turn it around.

The orange-yellow
The light green
The red, rather mellow
The best you've seen . . .

*Rebecca Mather (11)*
*Chepstow Comprehensive School*


# MY KALEIDOSCOPE

My kaleidoscope has an orange colour
*O r a n g e*

My kaleidoscope has a pink colour
*P i n k*

My kaleidoscope has a red colour
*R e d*

My kaleidoscope has a green colour
*G r e e n*

My kaleidoscope has the best colours
*B e s t!*

*Ceri O'Sullivan (11)*
*Chepstow Comprehensive School*

## WHAT ELSE IS BLUE?

The sky is blue
The sea is blue
The blue waves crashing
What else is blue?

The poppy is red
The fire is red
The red blood dripping
What else is red?

The grass is green
The tree is green
The green leaves blowing
What else is green?

The daffodil is yellow
The sun is yellow
The yellow banana on the tree
What else is yellow?

*Rachel Cross  (12)*
*Chepstow Comprehensive School*


## COLOUR THAT SHINES BRIGHT

Green is for grass - does it shine bright!
Red is for fire with it's light
Blue is for sky what a beautiful sight
With everyone watching
Getting a glimpse of the sun
*Moon and sky . . .*

*Vickie Phillips  (12)*
*Chepstow Comprehensive School*

## COLOUR

Drip go the raindrops
Clear as crystal
No colour there!
The sky we see blue as the sea.
Clouds as soft as pink candyfloss
Red and bright fires shine
Black smoke deepens the sky
Green grass as soft as cotton wool.
The grass so green you bounce
Upon it
The night sky with the bright stars
Stars very very bright
Light up in the night sky
Raindrops so
Clear
Say
Goodnight
Colour
Dear . . .

*Victoria Louise Daly  (11)*
*Chepstow Comprehensive School*


## COLOUR

Red is blood, fire and horrible things.
Blue is a fish, sea and sky.
Yellow is the sun and stars that twinkle at night.
Green is a tree and silky grass.
Pink is a rose and rosy cheeks.
A rainbow is all colours - it's a kaleidoscope . . .

*Paul Griffiths  (11)*
*Chepstow Comprehensive School*

## IMAGES OF COLOUR

The fire of a bonfire ferociously lit
Darting and swooping in the night sky.
Cracking and roaring the fire is dying.
The colour is rioting red . . .

Walking through the forest in late autumn,
Swishing my feet through the crispy leaves.
They're drifting down softly until they reach the ground.
The colour is bursting brown.

The sun is erupting
Shooting rays down to earth
The light is as dazzling as gold
The colour is yo-yoing yellow . . .

*Kathryn James  (11)*
*Chepstow Comprehensive School*


## COLOURS

Blue is the clear sky
Blue is the rough sea
Green is the long grass
Green leaves falling off the trees.

Yellow is a big juicy lemon
Yellow a sunflower - tall in the field
Grey is the sky when going to rain
Grey is paint on a wall.

Black is the colour that I like
Black is the colour of the night.
Orange is a small little orange
Orange is the colour of my book.

*Jonathan Moss  (11)*
*Chepstow Comprehensive School*

## FIRE, TREES AND SEA

The bright red fire
It was burning with a fright
Red, orange, and yellow
So bright it glowed in my eyes.

The trees twinkling so bright
The green stands out *really*
It is nice and bright
The leaves are all kinds of different
Yellows, greens and browns.

The sea is sparkling blue
It is shining from the sky
It stands out so bright
The waves make a whooshing noise!

*Keira Hughes  (11)*
*Chepstow Comprehensive School*


## COLOUR WAVES

Red the planet Pluto
Orange the sun
Silver the clouds above
And blue is the sky in day

As I look deep into the sky
I see an orange comet pass by
Is that the North Star I see?
Shining in all its glee!

As I look at the sea,
I see blue - blue I see

Saturn which is a mixture of colours,
Reds, pinks, blues - looks so nice,
Nice against the gloom . . .

*Hayley J Johns  (12)*
*Chepstow Comprehensive School*


## COLOURS

What is red?
A juicy apple
And blood too.

Green, what is green?
A blade of grass,
And leaves that fall
Off the trees.

What is yellow?
The bright sun
And a banana

Blue, what is blue?
The beautiful ocean
And so is the cloudy sky.

What is orange?
The sunset in the morning
A sour orange.

Silver what is silver?
The beautiful moonlight
Is silver . . .

*Kimberley Savage  (11)*
*Chepstow Comprehensive School*

## PEACEFUL SLUMBER

One day I looked into the bright blue sky
I saw a bird that spread its wings to fly.

He gracefully flew and soared all day long
Whilst other birds admired and sang their song.

I could hear the wind rustling through the leaves
So then I looked towards the nearby trees.

As I did so I caught a glimpse of yellow
Buttercups were dancing in the meadow.

So then I stopped, looked and admired the view
And I gazed in awe at the drops of dew.

Then peaceful thoughts began to fill my mind
I was thinking thoughts of every kind.

Once again I stared at the bright blue sky
Where white fluffy clouds were floating up high.

I then began to feel content and gay
As I drifted further, further and further away.

Then suddenly I awoke with a fright
To find it was the middle of the night.

All the beauty that I had seen
Had only been a beautiful dream.

The cold of the night put a shiver in my feet
But my warm thoughts were a tingling treat.

Those thoughts will stay
*. . . with me forever!*

It will not matter whatever
*. . . the weather!*

*Kristy Sanford  (13)*
*Fairwater Comprehensive School*


## MY HAMSTER

She is very small
with tiny feet.
She is coloured brown
loves peanuts and treats.

At night
in the wheel she goes,
Running and running
with her little pink nose.

She is quite tubby
with hardly no tail.
She is very fast
unlike a snail!

She's messy and naughty
on her back is a stripe,
She's very noisy
hasn't got a powerful bite . . .

*David Wells  (13)*
*Fairwater Comprehensive School*

# AREN'T WE LUCKY

Aren't we lucky
For getting everything today
Don't you think we're lucky
For having our own way . . .

Unlike some people
With relatives at war
Their lives are so traumatic
They can't take any more . . .

Some are so poor
They haven't any food to eat
They have no clothes to wear
Nor shoes upon their feet.

Just compare that to us
We have homes, warmth and food
We get everything we want
Depending on our mood.

*Hannah Price  (13)*
*Fairwater Comprehensive School*

## SHADWELL JONES

Shadwell Jones was a simple kid,
Who always did what he was bid.
Until the day his father died
Shadwell Jones had never cried.

Ever since that day had come
Shadwell Jones played in the sun.
Now he stays locked up indoors
His lonely head down in his paws.

As he grew from boy to man
Shadwell Jones had one fan.
That stuck by him through thick and thin
The pub
The only place to let him in.

He got old
No more the king.
Not of the land
But a boxing ring.

His time of end was very near,
Shadwell Jones had it worked out clear.
He knew that he was going to die,
To join his Dad up in the sky . . .

*Jennifer Morgan  (13)*
*Fairwater Comprehensive School*

# SUN LIFE

She rises, to a new day of joy,
filled with hope and despair,
laughter and happiness
sadness and grief.
The darkness she captures,
grasping it with her many beams.
I suddenly glance at her
rising over the hill.
Huge, colourful and bold.
Her magical mystery seems to smile at me,
warming my life, warming my heart,
making me smile.
But then, when the winter arrives,
darkness takes over with the moon as his partner.
Part of me feels sadness, the sun's disappeared,
But part of me feels joy, as next year the sun will
reappear,
laughing, singing, crying
watching darkness dying.

*Amy Davies  (13)*
*Fairwater Comprehensive School*

## WALES IN SPRING . . .

In Wales, mornings break - enveloped in misty smoke.
While the Welsh dew clings to plants and trees like a sparkling
diamond cloak.
Wales is like a passageful of broken dreams.
And old Welsh tales and memories are sewn in familiar
winding streams.
The things that represent Wales are daffodils, dragons and leeks!
While spring plants grow freely amongst the Welsh mountain peaks.
The sky is pearly white shot with shafts of peach.
Wales reaches a point of peace that some other countries can't reach.
The beauty of the soft golden springs in Wales are beyond and compare.
And the rosy light that caresses you is unmistakably Welsh and rare.
The day comes to an end - the sun finally cools.
As the lazy trout leaps half-way out of the Welsh reflecting pools . . .

*Amy Oates  (14)*
*Fairwater Comprehensive School*


## FOOTIE! FOOTIE!

I like to play football
If you are a goalkeeper it helps to be tall
There is 90 minutes in a game
If you are good - you will find fame.

My position is right back
But I would like to play in attack
If I keep my place in the team
I might be able to fulfil my dream . . .

*Owain Bradley  (11)*
*King Henry VIII School*

## DOESN'T SOMEBODY CARE!

I live in a family of five,
It's just like a beehive,
With a buzz, buzz here
And a scream, scream there.
Doesn't somebody possibly care.
I've got a brother and a sister too
I just don't know what to do!
A Mum and a Dad - it's just too bad,
That's why I'm always so so mad.
With a smack, smack here
And a whack, whack there.
Doesn't somebody possibly
... Care...!

*Tara Hall  (11)*
*King Henry VIII School*


## OWLS

The owl is a nocturnal bird.
It hunts at the dead of night.
Scanning the graveyard for his meal.
The voles, mice and rats don't stand a chance.
He has brilliant eyes and razor sharp talons
It swoops and takes a mouse and takes it back for the chicks.
They devour it bit by bit leaving scraps for the adults,
He goes for another meal at the dead of night.

*Tom Wood  (13)*
*King Henry VIII School*

## CONCEPT

Something is following me
alone, in the dark.
A shadow of pain,
cradled in evil.
Shuddering as we pass
the smouldering glare
called street lights.

It hunts, a remnant
of a bygone age,
crawling, sliding,
a social drop-out.
Adrenaline rises.
I scream in
despair, agony.

It has me
helpless, isolated.
I am smashed against
the wall of disaster.

*Edward Saunders (12)*
*King Henry VIII School*


## PEOPLE

People, people everywhere
running round the market square.

People here, people there
Gosh! There's people everywhere . . .

*Kayleigh Moeller (11)*
*King Henry VIII School*

# MY DOG

I have a dog
Who bites a log.
Toby is his name.
He loves to play games.
Toby loves to play with a stick
As long as it's nice and thick.
He is small and black
I walk him up to the mountain track.
On a hot summer's day his tongue hangs out
He likes to laze and lie about
He falls asleep whilst
His blanket is in
*a heap!*

**Gareth Staphnill  (12)**
**King Henry VIII School**


# THE DRAGON'S DEN

High up on a mountainside, deep inside a cave,
Lives a legend,
Huge in size, small in brain span,
Is the dragon, who is hiding away from the world,
He is 20 feet tall and 10 feet wide,
He's a natural tank!
His eyes are as red as fire,
His wings are as big as 1 thousand eagles.

**Stephen Carrett  (12)**
**King Henry VIII School**

## SILENT STARING

Somebody's watching,
Eyes bore in,
Like hot pokers,
Frozen now.
Not moving,
But watching,
Studying, scrutinising,
You.
One move
That's all,
Just one
And it's over.
Finished.
But who,
Who will take the risk?
You,
Or them?
Unbearable silence.
Loud nothing.

*Jeana Hollands (14)*
*King Henry VIII School*


## GHOSTS

Ghosts are really funny
I wish I could be like them . . .
To haunt someone would be cool
And to act the fool like them . . .

*Alan Jones (11)*
*King Henry VIII School*

# THE SEASONS

Winter is fun and exciting
Snowmen, lights, and Santa Claus.
Playing in the cold, cold snow
And opening your Christmas presents.
Spring is happy, new and fresh
New trees, animals and flowers.
Lambs are skipping in the meadow.
And the stream trickling in the forest.
Summer is hot for beaches and sand
For making sandcastles and fishing.
That's what I like to do in the Summer
Autumn is full of swirling leaves,
Brown, orange and crimson.
Hide and seek between the trees
And home to a roasting fire.

*Laura Potts  (11)*
*King Henry VIII School*

# THE SIMPSONS

Bart, Lisa and Maggie too
they all want to own Krusty's shoe.
Even though they love Itchy and Scratchy
but compared with Krusty
*They are rather patchy . . .*

*Richard Hunt  (11)*
*King Henry VIII School*

# SISTERS

Sisters, sisters - I've got two!
this means there's always a queue for the loo.
They borrow my make-up and my lipstick
sometimes I think they're a dip-stick.
They borrow my clothes and my shoes
then we don't know whose is whose.
We're always arguing - someone's in a mood
that's not fair - she's got more food.
That's not fair she's got more clothes and socks.
Oh look out! She's faking the chicken pox!
These aren't my tights - they fit my chest
Oh well! No need for a vest.
Sisters, sisters - they're not bad
But I haven't got a brother and I feel quite sad!

*Sjabena Sealy (11)*
*King Henry VIII School*


# THE SPIDER'S WEB

The silvery web glitters brightly at night,
The graceful spider waits patiently,
As the fly flies blinding into the web,
As much as the fly fights the tighter he gets,
Then he waits to be the main meal.

*Rhys Thomas Llewellyn (12)*
*King Henry VIII School*

## MY SISTER - THE ALIEN!

Imagine my mum's surprise,
When she gave birth to a baby with three eyes.
'Is it a girl?' she cried
'No! It's an alien' the midwife sighed.
The doctors all stood in despair,
As my mum looked on with a desperate glare.
It gave a smile and jumped a little,
As they all had a good poke and a fiddle.
My dad walked in,
And immediately fainted into the bin.
My brother and I stood with glee,
As we watched the alien wriggle free.
Up and out of the nurses arms
And onto my father's out-spread palms.
I gazed at the small alien,
While it pointed towards the sky,
The doctor shouted as it jumped and started to fly.
Up, up to the ceiling it flew.
Where it gave an almighty *'Atishoo!'*
Looking up we saw not one, but two big balls of slime,
Astonished as we were, the three eyes stuck to the ceiling
Were perfectly fine.
My dad stood up with a lump on his head.
*'Come on dear, lets get you home and into bed!'*

*Huw Gullick  (14)*
*King Henry VIII School*

# TEENAGE DEPRESSION

Trapped inside these four walls
Madness becomes real
Tender age in bloom
Tyranny and oppression
Just because I'm different
I am not one of you

Try and survive this, I know it's hard
I thought that I knew
You can't see my anger
Peace and love everlasting
Why are you putting up with this?
Spring is here again

Why did it happen to me?
Now I am older than I was
Teenage angst has paid off well
I am weak and you are strong
Feel the sun against your burning skin
I will never surrender to them

A feeling of hatred everywhere I go
Make your daring escape
The North Star stands alone in the sky
Alone on this cold night
Depression the ruling force
Oh well, never mind

*Huw Groucutt  (12)*
*King Henry VIII School*

## WHETHER THE WEATHER

Whether it's wet,
Whether it's dry,
Whether it's hot or cold.

You can have fun,
In the rain and the sun,
Whether you're young or old.

You can be happy,
You can be sad,
Whether the weather,
Is good or bad.

Don't feel down,
With the frost and the snow,
You can guarantee weather,
Will come and go.

*Racheal Lumpkin  (12)*
*King Henry VIII School*


## TIME

Your time is up my friend,
See you next time,
If there's time.
Not enough time,
Time is precious
Or was when there was time to count
The seconds, minutes, days years
Gone
Goodbye time!

*Stuart Phillips  (12)*
*King Henry VIII School*

## THE MAN WHO DIDN'T KNOW HOW

This is a story about a man,
A man who didn't know how
And if he doesn't know how to do it,
How could he? How can he? Why should he?
He can't.

One day I saw him trying to get his laces done,
And though he tried, how much
He tried, he just fell on his bum.

As he lay there on his bum
He thought to himself,
Why can't I? Why can't I?
Everyone else can but I can't
Why?

Then a voice came down from the
Heavens above and said,
'The reason for this is simple my friend
So don't be in a slum,
Keep your chin up high and don't be dumb
And don't ever fall on your bum.'

This is a story about a man
A man who did know how
And if he does know how to do it,
How good is he? How clever is he?
Why must he?
He can!

*Dani Thomas  (12)*
*King Henry VIII School*

## WHAT ARE YOU!

What are you? People ask,
They set you a difficult task.
You ask yourself many questions,
Of course you're open to all suggestions.
What colour are you?
Black, brown, white or blue?
What size are you?
Big or small?
How high are you?
Short or tall?
How big are your feet?
Big, medium or petite?
What food do you like or maybe not?
Do you like it cold or prefer it hot?
Do you swing from tree to tree?
Or do you fly like a bumble bee?
May I ask for your reply
I trust you not to tell a lie
Thank you for your co-operation
I shall value this information.

*Gemma Trickey (14)*
*King Henry VIII School*

## SPRINGTIME

How beautiful are the flowers in spring
Daffodils, snowdrops, bluebells blooming.
They glow like diamonds in the sun
I sit and stare admiring them.

*Vicky Batkin (13)*
*King Henry VIII School*

32

## Tunnel Of Death

Whirlwind of smoke compressing against my cold and softened face,
Figures and shapes unable to be identified.
As they curl through the white cloudy patches they glide towards me.
I feel my stomach jump with joy as they try to communicate,
They do not speak but yet I understand this is for eternity.

I come to an untouchable stairway,
Which somehow draws me,
But I know,
I know too well why they call me through.

I see these faces signalling for me to come,
But something just denies me the chance to go and rest.

*Jessica Hudson  (13)*
*King Henry VIII School*

## Fighting

Fighting is evil
Fighting is bad
You only fight when you get mad!

A fight can get very bloody
If you fight in the mud you get muddy
If you fight your way through life
You're going to end up in a bit of strife.

*Adam Phillips  (13)*
*King Henry VIII School*

# I'M ALL ALONE

Outside the wind is howling,
The shutters rattle angrily,
Spears of rain hit the roof,
It's dark, it's silent,
No light penetrates through the dusty window,
I'm all alone.

A floorboard creaks,
A door slams shut,
An icy chill runs up my spine,
I shiver,
The house once more is silent,
I'm all alone.

*Barley Blyton (12)*
*King Henry VIII School*

# HALLOWE'EN

Throughout the realms of dark and gloom,
There lies a house with one small room,
And in that room a paranormal crack,
But don't get too close you won't come back.
For once a person got too close,
When Hallowe'en night arose
This person never lived to tell,
Of the crack that led straight to Hell.

*Shani Viveash (12)*
*King Henry VIII School*

## SILVER

Slowly, silently now the moon
Walks the night in a silver shoe
This way and that she peers
And sees silver flock upon silver wool.
Now there suddenly was a garnish of silver jewels
On a silver crown.
Sailing down the silver dinghy.
So while we were playing with a silver draught
My friend Aulio felt a bit moodio.
While we were in a room luminous light
Shone upon my silver watch.
It was in my garden where I found some silver magnolia.
The singer, when he is on the silver mike
He guesses he does his dutio.

*Samuel Barnor (13)*
*King Henry VIII School*


## FOOTBALL

Football is so great,
It's a game of love and hate,
People passing to each other,
I don't know why they even bother.
Score a goal and you're a champ,
Miss a sitter and you're an old gramp.
Football is a game of skill,
It's a boring game if it finishes nil-nil!

*Jamie Laurent (12)*
*King Henry VIII School*

## THE MARY ROSE

The blue glittering sea on a sunny day,
The Mary Rose sails out proudly,
Great King Henry,
With his velvet and gold costume,
Went out on the castle wall,
To wave his ship goodbye,
But suddenly!
A huge tidal wave like a bully
Hit the ship from behind
And it toppled over like a skittle.
And it started to sink.
The soldiers were waiting,
As they knew they were going to die.
As the swirling water got nearer to them,
Wives, children, and lovers shed tears,
As the great ship disappeared
To the bottom of the sea.

*Neil Harris (12)*
*King Henry VIII School*


## THE BUG

It's smiling at me from over the grass,
A hairy back and eyes so enchanting,
I'll keep quiet I think, maybe it's hunting.
For another bug, with eyes still gleaming,
It hops from blade to blade,
And jumps when the blade starts leaning.
It hops so far it's out of sight,
Through the hedge and into a garden,
Out into the big wide world,
Out to stardom.

*Amy Talbot (12)*
*King Henry VIII School*

## THERE'S A GHOST IN MY BEDROOM

There's a ghost in my bedroom what shall I do?
Shall I go into my brother's room?
It's howling, it's hooting, it's scaring me.

There's a ghost in my bedroom what shall I do?
I know I'll make friends with it. Hello, hello
What is your name, please stop howling and hooting
It's scaring me. Can we be friends, please, please.
All I want is a good night's sleep.

There's a ghost in my bedroom what shall I do?
I'll ring the Ghostbusters to bust this ghost out of my room!
It's gone all quiet, I wonder why
Has the ghost gone for the night.

*Christopher Wenham  (12)*
*King Henry VIII School*

## THE ORCHESTRA

One hundred musicians playing in time,
The conductor holds the key,
Baton in hand swinging in time,
It all means something to me.

Quavers, semiquavers, crotchets alive,
The musicians play the tune,
Strings, brass, percussion, woodwind
Is where I want to be!

*Laura Lewis  (12)*
*King Henry VIII School*

# HALLOWE'EN FRIGHT NIGHT

At night there is afterlife, abnormal boils of blood.
Blood-stained bodies and bubbling cauldrons,
Cold churchyard coffins.
Dungeons and dragons, demons and devils.
Evil extraordinary eyeballs of fire
Foul fright.
Gruesome ghouls, ghosts and goblins
of Hallowe'en.
Horror and hatred of insiders and
icy imagination of jackals joo-joo
and jaws.

*Owen Carr  (13)*
*King Henry VIII School*

# FRIENDS

Friends
Friends are people who help you
Friends are people who care
Friends are people you talk to
Friends share
Friends are people you trust
Friends are people you can rely on
Friends are people who love you
Friends don't lie
*Friends need friends!*

*Lindsey Perry  (13)*
*King Henry VIII School*

## TITANIC

There she sails
Across the sea
'Titanic's unsinkable'
Says all of we.

Made of steel
Fit for a queen
But her future
Is yet unseen.

An iceberg is sighted
Stop the ship
Alarm bells ring
Must be quick.

The first class leave
On the lifeboats
But down below
The second class freeze in their coats.

People are screaming,
The last lifeboats leave
Over half the souls are left
It's hard to believe.

Down goes Titanic
The passengers freeze
Their souls lost
To the Atlantic sea.

*Ryan Griffin  (13)*
*King Henry VIII School*

## THE CAT ON THE MAT

The cat on the mat,
With its slick black mane
Eats Whiskas and tuna
With the Tom down the lane.

The wall is tall,
Like the tower in town,
Which stands in the lane,
By a house on the downs.

The house has a mouse
Which has bony knees,
A white shabby coat
And a fondness of cheese.

The moon like a loom
Spins a coat of light,
And moves around the earth,
Like a silver kite.

The stars by Mars
Twinkle bright up high,
As the cat looks up
With the Tom in the sky.

*Anna Gray  (13)*
*King Henry VIII School*


## MY CAT GINGER

My cat Ginger is as fluffy as a duster,
and as cuddly as a teddy bear.
He curls himself in front of the fire
like a ginger, contented python.
He's as ginger as a biscuit
and as sweet as he could be!

I love my ginger pussy cat
and I know he loves me too.
He purrs, he licks, he rubs my legs and
when playtime ends he follows me upstairs.
On my bed he lies on my warm feet
until morning time arrives.

*Hannah Davies (11)*
*King Henry VIII School*


## LOST

I am alone and frightened,
The night is cold
The grass is wet, my fur is damp,
The only sound is the beating
of my heart and the restless
whisper of the wind through the trees.
I curl up in an effort to get
warm but the cold penetrates
through my skin and sends a
shiver up my spine.

The moon shines, I am in the
spotlight.
I miaow, a single cry of misery,
I close my eyes and see my house
I almost feel the warm hand of
my beloved owner.
I open my eyes and reality
pours in.
A raindrop falls on to my face
As if it is a silent tear.

*Mary Maddocks (12)*
*King Henry VIII School*

## KALEIDOSCOPE

Pretty colours swirling round,
Red, yellow, green and blue.
Twist the eye-piece, and you'll have,
A completely different view!

And the shapes, ever moving,
Diamonds, squares, triangles too.
Give the end another twist,
What shape will it be for you?

Put them together
What do you see?
Shapes and colours,
Dancing free!

Life is a kaleidoscope,
Twisting round and round.
Always moving, never stopping,
Hardly ever touching ground.

*Briony Davis  (12)*
*King Henry VIII School*

## UNDER THE SEA

Under the sea
Is a new world to me
There are all different creatures to see
To see what you want
You've got to dive deep in the world beneath.

*Caron Griffiths  (13)*
*King Henry VIII School*

## THE EAGLE

The eagle so peaceful just sitting there,
Until it spots its prey,
The mouse is scuffling along the floor,
Without a care in the world,
Until the eagle rises up,
Flying through the sky,
Piercing the air like a dart.
The bird swoops down catching
The mouse in its sharp claws,
The eagle such an elegant bird,
In each and every way.

*Michelle North  (13)*
*King Henry VIII School*


## CREEPY THINGS IN THE NIGHT

Ghosts haunt you in the night,
Don't worry, they'll only give you a fright
Gnomes go round chasing kids
Don't go near them, or they will rip you to bits
Werewolves come out in the great moonlight
Don't worry, they'll turn human in the morning light
Vampires which come out for lunch
Don't be scared, just give them a punch
When you can see the morning light
You are safe for another night.

*Shirley Liu  (13)*
*King Henry VIII School*

## The Hunt

The hunt is on,
The men all shout:
Let's sound the song,
The fox is about.

Bring your guns
And weapons to kill,
The fox that runs
Over the hill.

Bang, bang, bang,
The fox is dead!
Hear the cheers that are said,
By the men dressed in red.

*Jonathan Edwards (13)*
*King Henry VIII School*

## A Disco

It's just begun
The lights are flashing
Red, yellow, blue
The music blaring
'I love you.'
You get up and dance
Now here comes your chance,
The boys coming over
But before you can ask
It's all over.

*Kirsty Hicks (13)*
*King Henry VIII School*

## A RAINY DAY

A great downpour rushed itself hard against my window.
I looked out of my window, such a gloomy day,
I was in my bed and that's where I lay.
What I would wish for it to brighten up,
More beaming blazing sun,
Then I could lie on the beach and have some fun.
I tried to get to sleep again.
A tapping noise was persistent on my window frame,
Then suddenly the keen sun came.
It seemed like a big bag had popped.
All of the daylight had come rushing out,
Piles of leaves flying about.

The leaves were dazzling everywhere,
They were like birds in the sky,
They would float about then fade and die.
The wet, damp leaves glistened in the sun.
So this is the rain and there's nothing we can do,
But the wildlife around us will see us through.

*Lorraine Somers  (13)*
*King Henry VIII School*


## GALAXIES

A swirling, whirling galactic magnitude of inter-stellar splendour.
All the spiralling mass of giant balls of rock and gaseous explosive
tremendousness.
Billions upon trillions of spherical lumps of elemental magnificence,
Down to the smallest microns, electrons, atoms or molecules,
It all amazes in awesome wonder the phenomenon that are galaxies.

*David Benson  (13)*
*King Henry VIII School*

# I SAW . . .

I saw a cloud crash down to earth,
I saw a car just about to give birth,
I saw a cow bungy-jumping off a bridge,
I saw the milk jump out of the fridge,
I saw the sun burst in the air,
I saw a worm with bright green hair,
I saw the moon, fall into doom,
I saw a tortoise suddenly zoom,
I saw my hamster riding a bike,
I saw my bed go on a hike,
I saw the world drop into space,
And now the world is a quieter place.

*Abby Forster (13)*
*King Henry VIII School*

# SCHOOL

School, school, school,
All it is, is one big rule.
We're all dressed in navy blue,
And you can't tell the difference between me and you.

During English, maths and French,
Some can sit on a bench,
Others have to sit on a chair,
Which are really hard and bare.

When we are in RE,
It's like being on safari.
All the kids are like animals,
Ripping up all the manuals.

Science class is always cool,
The only thing is that we have to sit on a stool.
The teacher is quite alright,
But I wouldn't mind blowing him up with dynamite.

*Christopher Davies (13)*
*King Henry VIII School*


## SMELLY FEET

I was walking down the street,
When, I smelt some smelly feet,
And I looked up and saw Elvis Presley.

So I took him in my car,
To a chemist not that far,
And I bought him some new odour eaters.

The odour eaters didn't work,
So I started the car with a jerk,
And took him to a new shoe shop.

The smell of his feet,
Smelt out the whole street,
And I jumped up and dragged him away.

Then I had a brilliant idea
I took him to the Weston pier
I pushed him in the sea
And was as happy as can be
As the smell drifted away from me.

*Anna Holder (13)*
*King Henry VIII School*

## A Sailor's Yarn

When I was younger,
I decided, through hunger,
That I was going to become a sailor.

For my wife, you see,
She never cooked my tea,
Even though I worked hard as a tailor.

So I got on a ship
And said 'Oh what a trip
I am going on to get some food,'
Then I realised that,
I'd forgotten my hat,
So then I was in a bad mood!

Then five minutes before,
We were due to leave shore,
My wife, she came running to me,
And from behind her back,
She produced my hat!
Then I was happy as could be!

So I gave her a kiss
And said 'Oh how I'll miss . . .
You and everyone else that I know!

*Nichola Cantle  (13)*
*King Henry VIII School*


## My New Computer

This is all too technical for me with *dram, vram, sram* and *ram*
This is not what was promised which was mainly *jam!*

*Eeprom* (Electrically Erasable Programmable Read Only Memory)
I am afraid that my brain is thinking only of food (*Chips and celery!)*

Complementary Metal-Oxide Semiconductor *(CMOS)*
Oh great! Time for tea. Now where's my *thermos?*

The only thing I know about this computer that's brand new
Is the *CPU!*

*Andrew Church  (12)*
*King Henry VIII School*


## COMPUTERS DON'T BITE

Some people say computers don't bite
But if they knew the truth they'd get a big fright.

In the middle of the night they come to life,
They creep outside the bedroom door and down the
stairs to the bottom floor,
They scare the dog and chase the cat round the
cupboard and under the mat.

Some people say computers don't bite
But if they knew the truth they'd get a big fright.

Catching a glimpse of all in sight they quietly move
into the night,
By now the computer's powers fade,
As they head towards where they were made,
They're undecided which way to go
Their power now is really low.
But then they find there is no way
So at last they decide to hit the hay.

Some people say computers don't bite . . . or do they?

*Robert Matthews  (11)*
*King Henry VIII School*

## THE SUN

The sun rises every morning
And gives us light and heat
It makes the plants and crops grow
So we have food to eat

We need the sun to work and play
It helps us every single day
I hope it never goes away
Or else we all shall have to pay

But when the night draws in
And the light begins to dim
The sun has gone away
Until another day.

*Alice Sidwell  (13)*
*King Henry VIII School*

## THE EAGLE

He clings to steep rocks
High in the sky.
He watches with his
yellow eyes.
Then, like a streak
Of lightning, he dives into
The sea all
foaming and white
Fish in his talons
Off he flies,
Back into the deep blue sky.

*Luke Llewellyn  (11)*
*King Henry VIII School*

## THE PALACE BALL

Last week in the palace hall
I had the most amazing ball.
At the beginning in the sky
I heard the most threatening cry.
By golly gosh it was the queen
Man she went down with a scream.
I quickly legged it out the back
Closely followed by an injured rat.
Then I ran up the stairs
Decorated with the skins of bears.
Along the corridor and around the bend
Oh heck oh horrors a dead end.
The king was on me like an eagle
Beside him a drooling beagle.
It pounced, I fell
Then came the gates of *hell.*

*Benjamin Callard  (11)*
*King Henry VIII School*


## BREAK AT SCHOOL IS VERY COOL

Break at school is very cool
We have football, ruby, cricket too
Sometimes I have pizza and chips
I'll go to the library to read and think
If it is wet we stay inside
To play Scrabble by the side
When it comes to two o'clock we all go *boo*
Because the bell goes *bring* and we all go in
And that's the end of break at school.

*Jon Bowen  (11)*
*King Henry VIII School*

# HEARTBEAT

I am the heart,
Pump, pump, pump, pump,
Pumping blood all day long,
Pump, pump, pump, pump,
Pumping blood,
Pump, pump, pump, pump,
To the organs that need blood,
Pump, pump, pump, pump,
Without me,
Pump, pump, pump, pump,
There would not be a you,
Pump, pump, pump, pump,
So please look after me,
Pump, pump, pump, pump,
Or I will disappear,
Pump, pump, pump, pump,
No smoking please,
Pump, pump, pump, pump,
No alcohol please,
Pump, pump, pump, pump,
No stop that,
Pump, pump, pump, pump,
You're choking me,
Pump, pump, pump,
You're making me dizzy,
Pump pump,
No, save me please,
Pump . . .

*Sarah Webster  (12)*
*King Henry VIII School*

## ARMY CADETS

*Drill*

Stand at ease, stand easy
Squad!
As you were
Squad!
As you were
Squadron

I hate drill, I hate it.
Every day we have to do it.
Right turn, left turn, about turn, every turn
My legs ache after a while
And I just can't stop laughing

*Drill*

Enemy
300m
Centre of ark
Lone tree
Watch and shoot

About turn
Enemy tank
Quadruple time
Quick march

Orders, orders
Boring orders
I prefer to go on my own

Probably I would die!

***Michael Hayward  (13)***
***King Henry VIII School***

## FUNFAIR PLEASE COME

You go through big gates
with all of your mates
into colourful lights
where there's a few fights
The waltzers go round
and make you dizzy
They sell lots of sweets
and drinks that are fizzy.
You can go on fast rides that are . . .
fun fast
twirly whirly
somersault
in the air
high low
here we go
hair in the air
*Oh no!*
The tagada is bumpy
and sounds very grumpy
With bruises on your back
You could give it a whack

The ghost train's dark
but where do you park?
It is all spooky
the roads go all loopy
because it . . .
pushes you
whooshes you
bangs you
clangs you
all over
the sides

The sky goes all dark
the music goes quiet
the rides are stopping
my eyes are closing
it's-time-to-go-to-bed.

*Louisa James  (11)*
*King Henry VIII School*

## WHO'S BILLY?

Our Miss James,
Took our names,
Because we had been silly.
So I said,
Mine was Fred,
Although it's really Billy.

So Miss James,
Never blames,
Anyone called Billy.
But instead,
She thinks Fred,
Is the one who's silly.

Now Miss James,
Often exclaims,
Fred - stop being a silly Billy.
And it's said,
She goes to bed,
Muttering - who on Earth is Billy?

*Martha Skilton  (11)*
*King Henry VIII School*

## THE SIMPSONS

Bart and Lisa off to school
in the mini bus for school
They got off by the bus stop by the school
Bart had his spray cans and his books
Lisa and her looks and books
while the kids were learning hard
Homer was drinking hard
Maggie sucking hard on her little pinky dummy
Marge was brushing up her hair getting ready for the fair
Mo was serving drinks to Homer while Bart's
on the phone,
Santa's little helper the dog and Snowball the cat
were fainting in the garden while Homer's lying dead.

*Leanne Hayes  (11)*
*King Henry VIII School*


## HALLOWE'EN

H  owls of werewolves make the night a big fright
A  bout in the graveyard there are ghost and bones
L  urking in the night a vampire is waiting
L  icking the blood off a bone is a werewolf
O  nly the luckiest people survive
W  hen the lights go out the ghouls come out
E  vening of revenge on the people that killed them
E  vening now comes to an end
N  ow all the ghosts and scary monsters go to sleep until next year.

*Daniel Holloway  (11)*
*King Henry VIII School*

## THE HOMELESS

Sounds of groaning and choking of
hungry, starving people fighting for their food.

The homeless people have nowhere to go
have no fancy clothes or food.

They sleep on the streets or in a shop door,
Sheltering from the world as much as they can.

They beg for money in the day,
Trying to get food to survive
And if they don't they will go hungry
for another day.

It's a hard life living on the streets,
Everyone's out for what they can get,
Having to watch your back wherever you go.

As they get older their bones grow weak and cold.
They start to get wrinkles that shred now and again
They start to cough and suddenly everything goes still
Lights go out and life has gone.

*Lucy Haskins  (12)*
*King Henry VIII School*


## THE HORSE

The horse galloped across the field.
His black glossy coat shining in the sun,
He jumped the fence around he reeled.
It was his favourite game and
He thought it was fun.

*Carly Regan  (11)*
*King Henry VIII School*

# POLAR BEAR, POLAR BEAR

Polar bear watching,
Polar bear silent,
Polar bear eating,
Polar bear quiet.

Polar bear running,
Running for its life
Polar bear running,
From a hunter's knife.

Polar bear crying,
Howling in pain,
Polar bear dying
Never to be alive,
Again.

*Kayley Hollands  (12)*
*King Henry VIII School*

# BLACK

The bomb explodes, all that is seen is black,
A boy dies, his name was Jack,
His sister cries, a baby born,
His family left, left to mourn.

Mother fades, fades to black,
Children cry, willpower they lack.
Strength of the living, weak of the dead.
All is brought from this colour black.

*Jessica Lloyd  (13)*
*King Henry VIII School*

## THEY'VE GONE

Questions circling my mind
Why had I been so selfish?
There's only me to blame.
Why?

If only I had known
That human hearts are sensitive
They're not made of stone,
Like the heart that belonged to me.

I treated them like nothing
And now they've gone away
My dreams and hopes are faded
My life has gone to dust.

*Emma Williams  (12)*
*King Henry VIII School*


## HOLIDAYS

H  olidays are full of fun,
O  n the beach and in the sun,
L  ovely weather is great too,
I  f the sun does not burn you.
D  isney is the place to go,
A  s long as the wind doesn't blow,
Y  ou'll see Minnie, Donald, Mickey Mouse, and be
S  ure to see the haunted house.

*Sarah Walbeoff  (12)*
*King Henry VIII School*

## DIVING WITH REDMAN

There I was under the sea,
With Redman looking after me.

A great heavy tank upon my back,
Of compressed air there is no lack.

Deep down we went until the pressure rose,
I had to clear my ears and nose.

Lots of corals and fishes too,
The queen of the sea all yellow and blue.

The file fish with their kissing snout,
Are my favourite the way they pout.

The barracuda with the frowning face,
Like a game of tag and chase.

'Redman, don't let that lobster bite!'
it could have been a ghastly sight.

Look at those little tiny shrimps,
And all those lovely whites and pinks.

There I was under the sea,
Thank you Redman for looking after me.

*Beth Harrison  (13)*
*King Henry VIII School*


## ROOMANIA (MY ROOM!)

This is my nation,
You need a passport for it,
You need one for out,
My own laws, my own religion,
Higher authority doesn't affect me,
I've got my legal rights.

Oh no! I'm under attack,
Up goes the wall,
Down go the hatches,
They got me.
It's time to chew the gruel.

*David Addis  (12)*
**King Henry VIII School**

## WHEN WILL IT COME TO AN END?

When will the world come to an end?
Who knows, who cares?
It drives me round the bend,
All it is, is a 3D circle,
Floating in mid-air.

It has a few countries,
A few seas as well,
It's very big,
But not as big, as you may think.

There are another eight planets,
But not as important as mine,
they don't have life on,
Or maybe I'm wrong.

From space,
It looks so small,
From a plane,
It looks so huge.

So, when will the world come to an end?
Who knows, who cares
It drives me around the bend.

*Eleanor Evans  (14)*
**King Henry VIII School**

## BONFIRES

The bonfire smelt of dampened bark,
As the flames shone in the dark,
As they grew they made more light,
Which glowed through the dark, black sky.

Bang! Bang! The bonfire went,
Up, up the flames were sent,
People threw things onto the fires,
From clothes to junk and even car tyres.

Once the bonfire had gone out,
There was nobody about,
No adults shouting, no children yawning,
There were just ashes left in the morning.

*Kit Russell  (12)*
*King Henry VIII School*


## OLD

Standing all alone
on a cold winter's day,
no one else around me
except small boys at play.

Thoughts run through my mind,
of how it used to be,
when I was small,
and the boys were chasing me.

Now I am old,
I think in my mind,
How the world has carried on,
and left me behind.

*Danielle Lamont  (14)*
*King Henry VIII School*

## SCHOOL

School is not everyone's favourite thing,
In fact it's quite boring.
You have to get up at 6, 7 or 8,
And heaven forbid should you be late.

Waiting at the bus stop in the wind and rain,
Getting ready to use my brain.
The bus pulls up,
And everyone piles in as quick as they can,
And there's our horrid bus driver, Dan.

We look around to find a seat,
And turn on the heaters to warm our feet,
As we pull away from the bus bay,
I think to myself here goes another school day.

I can see the school it's now in sight,
And there by the doors is Mr White.
His bald head gleaming, his trousers too short,
I think he's my dad's 'kinda' sort.

The bell goes for the start of school,
And there's my mate Chris being a right fool,
Pushing and shoving, shouting and screaming.
'Ha-Ha!' Mr White's seen him.
I don't wait to see Chris's fate
'Cos I don't want to be late,
I walk into the class and suddenly *'Pow,'*
School has definitely started *'Now!'*

*Philip O'Connell  (12)*
*King Henry VIII School*

## MY RAT

My rat is called Herby,
He's really very sweet,
He doesn't often show it though,
'Cos he'll nibble at your feet.

Sometimes he's quite smelly,
But I've gotten used to it now,
I clean him out once a week,
But it gets dirty again somehow.

Herby often runs around,
Along my bedroom floor,
But one day he got an idea,
And scrambled out my door.

Down the stairs one by one,
Little feet trying to run,
Dad's big slippers came plodding along,
Herby knew he wouldn't last long.

He shot into the air like a canon ball.
Past the dog and into a wall,
That was the end of Herby my rat,
Who fell on the floor and got eaten by the cat.

*Laura Cole  (13)*
*King Henry VIII School*


## LIFE

L  ife is a strange thing
I   n which you experience many things
F  ull of wonder and mystery
E  motions always changing.

*Hannah Brown  (12)*
*King Henry VIII School*

# HALLOWE'EN

A dark and stormy night
A werewolf howls.
You walk into the spooky
House then you begin to scream.
You hear a groan, you hear a scream,
A zombie walks at midnight.
You know you are at your doom,
Then a swoop and laughing appears,
It's the witch to cut you up
And put you in her boiling cup.
She adds a frog and then a slug,
She then begins her wicked words.
*Hubble, bubble, toil and trouble.*
But you have not gone that far yet,
Ahh, a ghost, you run for help.
A headless horseman walks down the stairs,
It then falls down to your feet.
A head rolls round on the floor,
Its eyes bulging, popping out.
You yell and screech and turn far away,
Straight into the zombie's lair.
The zombie roars and grabs for you,
You squeak, you kick but there's no chance for you.
You will be dead in a moment or two,
You don't want to be there
When the monsters come out.

*Owain Wood  (12)*
*King Henry VIII School*

## SPRING!

My favourite time of the year,
The baby lambs begin to cheer,
The daffodils start to bloom,
Life wakes up from winter's gloom.

No more frost, no more snow,
As the sun begins to glow,
Off it goes the wind and rain,
Now we feel the warmth again.

Birds fly back from far away,
How I've longed to see this day,
Swallows, swifts, redstarts too,
They're all so glad winter's through.

As buds appear on the trees,
Mum is cleaning on her knees,
Cupboards are turning inside out,
Nothing is left lying about.

My favourite time of the year,
We all begin to cheer,
Winter's gone, spring is here,
Now we know that summer's near.

*Siân Binns (12)*
*King Henry VIII School*


## THE CLOSING OF THE ZOO

The kangaroo and the wallaby
Were talking in the zoo,
Along came a giraffe, who said
'How do you do?'
Sid the snake was watching
Alongside the chimpanzee
As the monkey swung in his tree
Saying 'Hey look at me!'

Along came the zoo keeper
And said 'Shh, keep down that noise!'
'If the people hear you talking
You'll scare all the girls and boys'
But all the animals,
Laughed with such glee,
That the zoo was shut down,
Because of the jamboree!

*Cathy Hook  (14)*
*King Henry VIII School*


## FY MRAWD

Tall and thin,
  A stubbly chin,
Dark brown hair,
  An eerie glare,
Loving and kind,
  Out of his mind,
A manic driver,
  Never a skiver,
Really swotty,
  Very spotty,
Sometimes mean,
  Seldom clean,
Often smoky,
  Always jokey,
Ever busy,
  Occasionally dizzy,
Tremendously loud;
  Fy mrawd -
My brother.

*Jennifer Marshall  (14)*
*King Henry VIII School*

## WHITE CLIFFS

W hite as snow,
H ard as
I ce,
T owering the clear blue sea,
E ndless and threatening.

C rumbling but proud
L ifting up from the sea.
I mmense and
F orceful,
F ighting to hold back the ravenous
S ea.

*Steph Turnbull (11)*
*King Henry VIII School*


## FIREWORKS

Fireworks, sizzling, screaming, up into the air.
Bangers bursting, racing to the ground with rage.
Flashes of light here and there.

The fire burns and crackles.
The night is cold but the flames are hot.

*Charlotte Prosser (13)*
*King Henry VIII School*

# TORNADO

The dot in the distance,
Barely visible to the naked eye.
As it comes closer,
The roar of the turbo fan engines can be heard.
The object becomes identifiable as,
A Tornado GR3.
The wings swept back as it,
Flies over at supersonic speed,
The roars of its engines following like a shadow.
The outline of the external fuel,
Tanks against the sky are breath-taking.
As it carried on going, it banks with such
Grace and beauty that it reminds me,
Of a falcon in flight.
As it heads off into the distance,
All becomes quiet.
The Tornado is just a speck against the clouds.
I wonder what the pilot was thinking,
As he flew over my head.

*Christopher Hill (14)*
*King Henry VIII School*


# ALIENS

Little green men,
Dancing on Mars,
I wonder if they're watching us,
Have they seen 'Mars Attacks'
or even 'Men In Black?'
Are they evil and mean,
Or just cute and fairly thick?

*Verity Turner (15)*
*King Henry VIII School*

## HOPE

Screams and cries of agony and pain
Swelled the death polluted atmosphere.
The continuous drown of their machine guns
And the devastating mutilated bodies from the bombing.
All became an oblivion
As my vision faded in and out.
And the noise fell on my deafened ears
I could feel the tight grip of my life
Loosening and slipping away.
How could I ever survive?
Did I really want to survive?
My lasting thought,
Is hope a thing for the optimistic
Or just the foolish.

*Jackie Watkins  (15)*
*King Henry VIII School*


## DIFFERENT

Not special, but strange.
Unfamiliar and outstanding.
I see these thoughts in your eyes.
You judge me without knowing me.
I am an alien to this country
and your system is unacquainted to me.
It is not easy for me to change my way of life,
But I have no choice.
You have always been here.
I am in a new country living in a foreign family,
Speaking to foreign people in a foreign language.
I am alone.

*Elizabeth Hobson  (14)*
*King Henry VIII School*

## SAVE MY POEM!

I write this poem,
As a plea,
Against the people
Publishing it for me.
They earn money
From my hard work,
It must be funny,
I can see them smirk.

The publishers
That's how their names goes,
That take my poem
From under my nose.
Then charge me cash
To read their trash,
I'd rather my work
Went up in smoke.

Vanity publishing,
It is called.
My poem's soul,
They tear it bald.
The worst thing is
They say it'll help.
The idea does
Make my poem yelp.

*Martin Adams  (14)*
*King Henry VIII School*

## MY SPECIAL LAND

My special land is purple pig,
I go there every evening.
You don't need a car or bus or plane,
You don't need a bike to get there.

My special land has orange trees
and multi-coloured flowers,
And in the sky are lemon bees,
Who fly around for hours.

My special land is upside down,
You walk round on the ceiling
And in the biggest town of all,
there's such a lovely feeling.

My special land is very close,
You can go there too.
Just close your eyes and fall asleep,
and you will be there soon.
It might not be my land though,
you can dream one of your own.
I'm sure you will enjoy it,
So go ahead just have a go.

And when the morning sun streams in,
and mother shouts 'It's school time'
My special land is wrapped away,
and out of bed I climb.

At half past three when I come home,
I know my land is near,
and when I climb in bed at night,
it all becomes quite clear.

*Steven Caswell  (12)*
*King Henry VIII School*

## THE FALLEN FLOWERS

An old man watches the parade
wearing his bright red poppy,
Silence at the eleventh hour of the eleventh day
of the eleventh month,
A young boy dressed in black giggles,
His mother gives him a nudge,
All is quiet,
One minute gone, two minutes,
The cornet plays 'The Last Post',
The soldiers and widows stand around the cenotaph,
They look so sad,
They place red wreaths gently down,
The vicar reads a prayer
Silence!

*Laura Terry  (12)*
*King Henry VIII School*


## I SHOULD LIKE TO PAINT

I should like to paint the sound of football fans
cheering after a goal,
I should like to paint the patter of ants' feet on the ground,
I should like to paint the sound of dust falling through the air,
I should like to paint the sound of joy at Christmas,
I should like to paint the sound of music,
and I should like to paint the sound of an animal's imagination,
I should like to paint the sound of the ocean in its great depths,
I should like to paint the sound of the trees whispering,
And I should like to paint the sound of the dead.

*Peter Chater  (11)*
*King Henry VIII School*

## ABANDONED

Why did you leave me,
  Cold and alone?
I don't know how I will survive,
  Now I'm on my own.

Why did you go away,
  Never to return?
Taking all the love,
  That we once shared.

Why did you abandon me,
  Without saying goodbye?
All those happy memories,
  You left behind.

Looks don't touch me,
  I cannot live.
Without the love,
  That you won't give.

*Khwanyo Bu  (14)*
*King Henry VIII School*


## AUTUMN

A  cascade of leaves fall from the trees,
U  p-turned noses at the sight of these.
T  he conkers are shiny, brown and polished,
U  nder trees soon to be demolished.
M  any foods for harvest time,
N  ow you can see the autumn signs.

*Alys Cottom  (12)*
*King Henry VIII School*

## THE RIVER

I went for a walk one evening
Down to the riverside
The perfect place for relaxation
And to watch the evening tide

The moon glinted on the ripples
And the leaves rustled in the breeze
This could be a dream I thought
And I'd dance around the trees

I knew this was no dream
For I'd come here to get away
From shouting matches that claim
To have serious results one day

The pressures of life slowly ease away
As I lie on the bank of the river
I gaze up at the stars above
And feel the cold that makes me shiver

This is a moment I want forever
But I can feel it slipping away
The clock strikes twelve, I slowly get up
And I feel light as a feather

Now I go back to family pressures
And for a moment I feel sad
But then I remember tomorrow always comes
And I'll come back again to the river.

*Fiona Bennett (14)*
*King Henry VIII School*

## THE VIOLIN PLAYER

He stands upon the stage all dressed in black,
While everybody waits.
The tent is filled from front to back,
While everyone debates,
What will he play?
How will it sound?
What will we say
To all around?
At last he picks up
His violin and bow.
As some people start to leave,
Until they hear him play so slow.
You could hardly believe,
That a violin and bow,
Could make such a noise
With a beat which does flow,
And he plays with such poise.
His music brings life,
To an instrument with strings,
Which happiness it then does bring.
So if you ever hear this sound,
Then you will know who to blame,
It is all down to the innocent sound
Of the magnificent violin player.

*Siân Eve Goldsmith  (14)*
*King Henry VIII School*

## SEASONS

The crystal-like snowflakes
Drift slowly down,
Down onto a flawless blanket of white.
And inside the house,
Quiet as a mouse,
A light shows a child
Sleeping through the night.

The moles wake up,
Up to the warmth,
Where birds spread their wings
And seedlings are sprouting,
And love birds pouting,
For the first kiss of spring.

The summer sun shines hotly from above,
Showing children playing
And donkeys braying,
Ice-creams melting,
And sun bathers sweltering.
The fun of the fair,
Showing everywhere.

The nights grow darker,
The stars twinkle brightly.
Showers of leaves
Fall from the trees,
In colours beyond imagining -
Russet, chocolate and gold,
Swept around out of control,
As the cold winds start to blow,
And autumn takes hold,
Of this beautiful changing world.

*Sian Robins-Grace (12)*
*King Henry VIII School*

## THE SEASONS POEM

I really like the winter
You can snuggle up inside
With warm fires glowing
In the darkness of the night

I really like the spring
The frisky lambs in the fields
And the daffodils brightening up every bank

I really like the summer
Even though it's hot
Sitting on the beach and making sandcastles
Or eating cold ice-creams

I really like the autumn
It is great to watch the happy, glowing faces
Of children stamping through crisp, crunchy leaves
Or collecting shiny conkers.

I really like the winter
You can snuggle up inside
With warm fires glowing
In the darkness of the night.

*Victoria Bowen  (13)*
*King Henry VIII School*


## A MADMAN

In LA there was a man with a sawn-off shotgun,
Everybody started to run,
He was blowing everyone away,
They said he was drunk he was in the pub all day,
Then he suddenly went skits and blew everyone to bits.
The police tried to stop him,
But they couldn't hold him down.

Now he shot a cop,
They said this must stop.
A copper punched him in the face,
Then the man pulled the trigger.
That's when the cop's body splattered all over the place,
Suddenly he ran out of ammo,
Then the cop went *kablammo,*
That's when the man was dead,
the cop shot him in the head.

*Wayne Llewellyn  (12)*
*King Henry VIII School*


## THE FIGURE

The boy rose slowly,
Up from the chair
Not making a sound.
As if by magic,
He hung in mid-air,
His eyes shut tight.
In the gloomy light the boy looked almost white.
The boy drifted slowly across the room,
Going out through the window,
Soon he would meet his doom.
The ghostly figure came up from behind
It was then that the boy opened his eyes.
The boy opened his mouth but no sound came out.
The figure laughed,
Then smoke, everywhere.
When the smoke cleared
The boy was gone,
Who took him? Where has he gone?

*Jonathon Ruck  (14)*
*King Henry VIII School*

## My Family

My mum is a pain, I think she's insane!
She goes in a mood, she won't make me food,
I go in a strop, she sneers at me a lot.

My dad is mad, but I like him a lot
My dad says go out, but my mum says I cannot.
I hate both my brothers, they annoy me all the time.

As you can see I wrote this poem in rhyme.

One of my grandfathers is dead,
He died when he was sleeping in his bed,
My other grandfather is funny
It's even better when he gives me some money.

My grandmother is really great,
She makes really good cakes.

*Kieran Shevlin   (12)*
*King Henry VIII School*


## Pirates

Pirates sail the Seven seas
Pirates have wooden knees
Pirates laugh with a ha, ha, ha
and they shout 'East ye land lubers
Yes you with the car.'
Pirates come in all shapes and sizes
Some have a patch on their eye
With the Jolly Roger flying high on the mast
Their wooden ship will sail fast
So beware when you go on the ferry
Because the pirates will be there ever ready.

*Gareth Pritchard   (12)*
*King Henry VIII School*

# I SHOULD LIKE TO PAINT

I should like to paint a cloud's thoughts
as he bubbles across the sky.

I should like to paint a flower's screams
as she is whisked up in the lawnmower.

I should like to paint the sun's sounds
as she rises in the morning for another long day.

I should love to paint a fish's thoughts
as she ripples in and out the coral in
a tropical seabed.

I should love to paint a tree's feelings
as he grows a beautiful new bud.

I should love to paint a kitten's feelings
as she chases a butterfly across the lawn.

I should love to paint a bird's happiness
as he grows a new blue feather.

I should love to paint a mother of pearl's
feelings as she is strung onto a necklace.

I would love to paint a crab's sadness
as he is served up for starters in a restaurant.

I would love to paint a fairy's feelings
as she collects the last tooth for her castle.

I should love to paint the world's feelings
as she sees how beautiful it is.

*Rhiannon Price (11)*
*King Henry VIII School*

## PRESSURE IN THE COCKPIT

The date is the 1st of October,
You are 9 points behind the championship leader,
The leader has been disqualified,
Only a win will do.
Pressure.

The last race of the season,
If you win, you will be world champion,
If you finish second or lower, you will be the runner up,
Sixteen races worth of hard work will have been wasted.
Pressure.

Pole position on the grid,
People wanting to spoil the party behind you,
Overtaking is virtually impossible at this circuit,
A good start is essential.
Pressure.

The red light comes on,
You gingerly press down the left gear lever,
Neutral has been engaged,
You hope your gearbox will not fail you.
Pressure.

Your left foot gently presses on the clutch pedal,
Your right foot resting on the accelerator,
All the lights come on, don't jump the start,
Don't mess this championship up now.
Pressure.

Your stomach feels heavy,
You fight to grab your nerves,
The lights have gone out,
You brace yourself, and you hope!

You have stalled. The championship is gone.

*Christopher Shephard  (13)*
*King Henry VIII School*

## I HOLD YOUR HEART

I hold your heart in my hands,
Unsure if I can continue pumping.
You gave me your heart
and if I let go I know it will break.

I hold your heart in my hand,
Hoping that soon I will be sure.
You depend on my support,
and if I no longer give,
I know it will grow weak.

To love and to last,
both hearts must pump for themselves,
dependant on no one's assistance.
To love and to last,
both hearts must stay strong,
lifted but not carried by love.

I hold your heart in my hand,
Weighed down by your clinging.
I pump with aching fingers,
wondering if your hands would tire easier.
My love for you fading,
I know I can't go on.

*Jo Iles  (14)*
*King Henry VIII School*

## IT'S NOT MY IDEA?

I imagine our future to be effortless,
technical machinery outdoes human assistance.
We will no longer need the use of Earth vehicles,
we'd take to the air in up to the minute spacecrafts.

Up there, anything's possible!
You could explore the outer limits,
take a tour of the planets,
Venus, Mercury, Pluto, Mars,
or even stick with the boutiques.

I, myself prefer the real world,
our Earth.
it keeps my feet firmly on
the ground . . .

*Hayley MacDonald  (14)*
*King Henry VIII School*


## I KNOW A BOY CALLED ADAM

I know a boy called Adam
He is very nice.
He is sexy, he is sweet
I think of him all night.
His face is very sweet
I like him very much.
If I got to know him
I like to keep in touch.
If I had the chance
I'd wrap him in a rug and
Keep him to myself.

*Lesley Date  (12)*
*King Henry VIII School*

# I SHOULD LIKE TO PAINT

I should like to paint the painter's brush wipe on
the canvas,
I should like to feel a painter's imaginations
as he puts his brush to paper,
I would like to hear the sound of the past
Or paint the liberty of life,
I should like to paint a bird as he flies through the clouds,
The glow in a tiger's eye on a very dark night,
I would like to paint the chase of a cheetah as he
catches a baby buffalo,
I should feel the happiness of a thrush as he is
warmed by the sun,
I would like to hear the hyena's hysterical laugh
as it dies into the night.

*Peter Mullen (11)*
*King Henry VIII School*


# HALLOWE'EN

At Hallowe'en spooky things happen,
ghouly ghosts come and haunt you,
grim reapers come and stalk you,
witches fly past your window at night,
zombies smash your window and give you a fright,
with pumpkins in their hands,
scarecrows with their fangs,
they're all coming,
but be careful,
they won't make a sound,
so goodnight and God bless and watch you don't fall into a
Hallowe'en nest.

*Rhys Watkins (11)*
*King Henry VIII School*

## I SHOULD LIKE TO PAINT . . .

I should like to paint the silvery scream of a shooting star
as it whizzes across the moonlight sky.

I should like to paint the dark and light of a golden
eagle's eye.

I'd like to see the bumble bee's buzz, as he sits upon a leaf.

I should like to hear the tiger's stripes and his sharp glistening teeth.

I'd like to see the wind's colour as he howls in at my window.

I'd like to paint a cat getting ready to pounce, crouching low.

I'd like to hear a deer's leap as it gallops through the wood.

I'd like to hear a blossoming rose bush I would if only I could.

I'd like to paint a willow tree sweeping across the floor.

I'd like to hear the little pips of a damp and soft apple core.

*Catherine Perkins  (11)*
*King Henry VIII School*


## TREVOR

Trevor, Trevor, not very clever,
Couldn't even count to ten.
He went to school,
But they called him a fool,
So he never went there again.

*James Matthews  (15)*
*King Henry VIII School*

## PURRFECT

He has a body so agile and sleek,
Pouncing and jumping in giant leaps,
Emerald green eyes and delicate paws,
Tiptoeing silently over the floor,
Purr, purr.

Head in the air so graceful and proud,
He's seeking attention by purring aloud,
Soft, black fur against my skin,
Affection coming from within,
Purr, purr.

Gliding along, walking thin,
Sleeping fat and eating in,
Always trying hard to please,
I love him dearly because he's
                    Purrfect.

*Holly Bryant  (12)*
*King Henry VIII School*


## I SHOULD LIKE TO PAINT

I should like to paint the sun sparkling in the sky
I should like to paint the squeak of a mouse
as it scurries for food.
I should like to paint a winter's morning as
snow is falling.
I should like to paint the night's sky.
I should like to paint the rain falling from the sky.
I should like to paint the landscape.
I should like to paint the sound of a drum as it is beaten.

*Kevin Carr  (11)*
*King Henry VIII School*

## HALLOWE'EN

Moan, groan and rustle,
The witches are coming, the witches are coming,
They cackle, swoop and make you scream,
Their hideous faces will make you turn green.
They gather round the cauldron chanting
'Hubble, bubble, toil and trouble.'
Growl, roar and rip,
The monsters are coming, the monsters are coming,
With six arms and seven feet,
They creep through the night hunting for meat,
Hiding in the shadows,
Hiding under beds,
You'd better be wary or you'll end up dead.

Witches on the rooftops,
Monsters eating meat,
It's All Hallows Eve
When the dead rule the street.

*Alex Busby (12)*
*King Henry VIII School*


## THE FIGHT

Fire-breathing dragon,
Its breath a fiery glow.
With scales on its back,
Be careful where you go!

A knight in shining armour,
Swords and lances,
One, two, three,
Battle commences.

The knights shining sword,
Flashes in the sun,
But then it shines no more for,
The knight cries my deed is done.

And the crowd cheers and shouts,
The dragon is dead,
The dragon is dead,
Well done!

*Kate Spooner  (12)*
*King Henry VIII School*


## BEAUTIFUL CREATURE HERE TO STAY

Padding silently through the dark,
The black beast seeks its prey,
Feared by all and everything,
That gets in this animal's way.
Her eyes shine brightly like head lamps,
Her huge paws make no noise at all,
This beautiful creature will search
From dusk all night right through till dawn.
This creature is more powerful than humans themselves,
It could chase you all right through a storm,
Her agile body not weary at all.
For she is still in quite good form,
This creature the panther,
So powerful and strong,
May care well for her cubs,
But for us, not at all.

*Louise Griffiths  (13)*
*King Henry VIII School*

## I SHOULD LIKE TO PAINT . . .

I should like to paint the sound of a monkey
sleeping in the dark, silent rainforest.
The sound of a lion snoring in his sleep.
I should like to paint the rustling sound of
hunting animals at night.
The sound of a car saying *beep beep.*

I should like to paint the wind howling on a
winter's night.
The booming and crashing sound of thunder
and lightening.
I should like to paint the sound of an earthquake,
which everybody would think so frightening.

I should like to paint the sound of a snail
moving ever so silently.
The sound of a cat purring ever so politely.

*Rachel Page  (11)*
*King Henry VIII School*


## THE WIND

Have you ever stopped to wonder,
How the wind is made?
Some people like it,
Some people don't.
It echoes amongst the trees,
Rustling and whistling,
And it is like a hidden force,
Invisible to me.
The wind will move the shutters,
Rustle the blinds,
And carry leaves from town to town.

Have you ever wondered,
How the wind is blown?
Is it a giant cloud huffing and puffing,
Or a giant fan?
Either way,
Day by day,
The wind is there,
The invisible force,
Stronger than the strongest man.

*Jonathan Woolley (12)*
*King Henry VIII School*


## A TIGER

Carefully strolling through the tall, dry grass.
Eyeing up his unsuspecting prey,
his eyes watching like a hawk.
Orange flames dancing with excitement.
The black stripes digging down like daggers.
Stooping low, its slender coat, shining
in the hot sun.
Sharp and long, its claws dig deep
on his face, a smirk, already.
Does he know that victory is his?
His long, bushy tail, swaying back and forth.
Waiting with anticipation,
to pounce at any moment.
Gleaming teeth,
ready for the kill,
lower and lower he stoops,
ready,
*grrr!*

*Jeni Stokes (13)*
*King Henry VIII School*

# FRIENDS

There's Rachel, Phoebe, Chandler and Ross
There's Joey, and Monica who in the house is boss
Phoebe's a hippy, a masseuse for her job
Joey's an actor, but only earns a few bob.
Monica's a chef at the local restaurant
She's not very popular but they're bound to come round.
Ross has a job as a palaeontologist
Something with dinosaurs, I think that's the gist.
Rachel's a clothes fitter at Bloomingdales
There she fancies one of the males.
These six people are all best of friends
Chandler is stunning but Joey's OK
They hang out at a cafe called Central Park
The coffee's OK, but Gunther's a jerk
They're like one happy family they get along well
Though there is still some tension between Rachel and Ross.

*Marion Lewis  (12)*
*King Henry VIII School*


# HALLOWE'EN

Hallowe'en is coming near,
Kiddies dressed up, with no hope of fear.
Ghouls and ghosts, witches on broomsticks,
Cauldrons bubbling, bats hanging.
Dracula's waiting for a glass of blood,
Skeletons walking bones clicking.
Hallowe'en is about fear.

*Charlotte Price  (13)*
*King Henry VIII School*

## SPLIT, SPLOT, INK BLOT

I sit here, daydreaming,
*English!*
Teacher mumbling,
This! That! Whatever . . .
Notes passing,
Pens scratching,
Trying to think of something to write.
Split, splot, ink blot.
Sitting there - in the centre of the page.
The mark.
My only words.
'Uh oh' teacher
Walking over.
'Vicki'
'Whay! Yes! What? (good start)
'What's that?'
'Split, splot, ink blot.'
(Very creative, don't you think!)
I thought I was a gonna.
Miss shook her head and walked away.
Split, splot, ink blot.
Why did I write that?
I don't think I did!
My pen has magic powers -
It even takes off its own lid.
Oh well, back to work!
*Split, splot, ink blot.*

***Victoria Griffiths  (12)***
***King Henry VIII School***

## THE ANIMAL KINGDOM

There are all sorts of animals
They are all shapes and sizes
Some are scaly and some are wet
And some are as cold as ice is.

One of the animals is a bumble bee
Who is very, very busy
If you look at them hard enough
You'll find you'll soon get dizzy.

Another of the animals is a dog
This is one of my favourite creatures
With his black eyes staring up at me
This is one of his best features.

*Donna Assirati  (12)*
*King Henry VIII School*


## SPACE

I'm flying through space,
No wind to move my hair,
I feel like a king.
Whizzing round and round,
No people to annoy me,
No need for clothes or money.
But without my friends,
There is no fun whizzing up and down,
Eventually only boredom and even insanity.
Now I want to go home,
Cuddle up in the warm,
And see my mum and laugh with my friends,
I want to have my fun back.

*Rhys Harris  (12)*
*King Henry VIII School*

## THE VAMPIRE

Everything is quiet, the sun's gone down
Everyone has gone to bed, there's nobody around.
The moon is out, sharp and bright,
She lights up the starry sky.
If people knew who was coming to kill
Who, and how and why?
By day it hides up in the skies,
By night it comes to terrorise.
Swooping through the crisp, cold air.
It needs to be killed, but nobody dares.
It targets a nice plump, juicy little boy,
Peacefully sleeping, or playing with his toys.
It brings out a file and sharpens its teeth.
Brings out a mirror checking its hair.
It's ready to kill but he really doesn't care.
Targeting its victim and swooping down low,
It can't wait to taste blood as it climbs the window.
Creeps over to the boy dreaming silent and sweet.
This creature's a guy you don't want to meet.
It takes this boy's plump little arm.
Doesn't it know that it's causing great harm?
It sinks its teeth in nice and deep
The little boy screams, but it's gone!
What a creep!
It's taken its daily dose of juicy blood.
You never know that because it's gone free.
One day this strange creature might come for you or me!

*Becky Robertson  (13)*
*King Henry VIII School*

## MUSIC

CDs, cassettes, music galore
all around the shops on every floor.
Classical to pop
Beethoven to 'Steps'.
Everyone has favourites
from folk to rock 'n' roll.

The charts are changing every week
to get people dancing to different beats.
You buy the CDs
to make them number one.
It's all a competition, but sometimes just for fun.
Some people make it to the top
and some fall down.

Songs are played at discos.
Bands play live on tour.
Music is a big business
changing all the time.

*Natalie Davies  (12)*
*King Henry VIII School*

## ORANG-UTAN

Does he know who his mother is?
  I wonder if he remembers
Is she dead or is she alive?
  I wonder if she remembers.

Will she enjoy breeze on her face
  As autumn turns to winter soon
Biting wind slaps his crumpled brow
  As autumn turns to winter now.

While climbing free in treetops above
Do you think she can recall him?
All alone he sits huddled up
Do you think he can recall her?

His eyelids close, a tear rolls down
  Why does he do it, why does he?
Do we have to run zoos this way?
  Why do we do it, why do we?

*Tristram Hall  (13)*
*King Henry VIII School*


## TEENAGERS

What is a teenager?
Someone who's between the age of 13 and 19
A troublemaker, a swat, a bully, a friend.
Or somebody who enjoys having fun.
Staying out late and getting drunk.
They shout at their parents 'cos they're being 'tight'
Won't let them wear make-up or go to the disco.
'You're not going out wearing that, or you're not
staying out till that late, I don't like your friends.'
That's all they ever say.
We don't like school, we think it's rubbish.
We love TV, music, boys/girls. It's normal.
Hanging out in a big gang of friends.
Supporting a football team.
We have a right to do what we want!
We have our own fashion
We have our own language.
They say 'Speak properly. It's think not fink.'
But we don't care, that's just what a teenager does.

*Cari Silcox  (13)*
*King Henry VIII School*

## RAINFOREST POEM

R ainforests around the world are very endangered.
A nimals are getting killed for their meat or skins.
I nsect species are wiped out through forest fires.
N ature is very important to the environment, and everyone
  should be aware of this.
F orests are very important to people, but they do not realise
  that it is important to animals too.
O nly with everybody's help we can avoid the destruction
  of the rainforests.
R eviving the rainforests is impossible to do without your help.
E verybody says that animals will survive but how can they when
  trees are being cut down or burned?
S ave the rainforests, and think about the animals living in the
  rainforests when you are cutting the trees down.
T rees are all important in the rainforest to form a canopy in which
  the plants and creatures can survive.

*Billie Prangley  (11)*
*King Henry VIII School*




## A LONELY BOY

There was a little boy
He had dark blond hair and brown sad eyes
His arms were just skin and bone
He barely ate at all
Everyone took the mickey out of him
Nobody cared that he was poor
He was never seen happy.

*Rhos Williams  (12)*
*King Henry VIII School*

## CUT OFF YOUR HEAD

I was asleep with my head on my bed,
When a deep voice said 'You're dead, you're dead, I'm gonna cut
                                                    off your head.'
I woke with a fright and I saw a startling sight,
There was a boy with his head cut off at the bottom of my bed,
To my surprise he said, 'You're dead, you're dead, I'm gonna cut
                                                    off your head.'
He raised his left hand and decided to stand,
There was a swift silent blow and a ho, ho, ho, and I was dead.
A few days later in my mum's room
There I was at the bottom of her bed with my head cut off and I said,
'You're dead, you're dead, I'm gonna cut off your head.'

*Gareth Thomas (12)*
*King Henry VIII School*


## HALLOWE'EN NIGHT

It was 31st October and trick-or-treaters aplenty,
Frankensteins, Draculas and lots of hideous monsters.
There was a young girl who got quite a fright for, a boy dressed
                                                    as a zombie
Lunged at the girl. She screamed and she cried and then ran away home.
A boy dressed as a mummy - he looked kinda funny,
Wrapped in toilet paper, he stumbled and fell.
A little Frankenstein mumbled and grumbled and knocked on the doors,
The little Dracula sat chewing his sweets.

*Thomas Folan (12)*
*King Henry VIII School*

## A GHOST CALLED JAKE

In a haunted castle long ago,
A friendly ghost did roam,
This is a sad tale of woe,
About this place the ghost called home.

There were lots of other spooks inside,
That were so very mean,
This poor ghost would try to hide,
Because they would make him turn quite green!

This little ghost called Jake,
Was bullied by the rest,
They scared him with a snake,
And all thought they were best!

One day Jake found a way,
To get rid of all the rest,
A plan using bales of hay,
To make him turn out best.

Jake first covered the gang in glue,
Then in lots of hay,
A simple plan that we could do,
And Jake shouted out 'Hooray!'

But the gang just threw him out,
And clipped him round the ear,
They said, 'Ungrateful little lout!
That's the last of us you'll hear!'

Jake floated off to his grave,
And wished that he could hide,
Then he did something very brave,
And disappeared inside.

That was the end of little Jake,
He's tucked inside his grave.

*Robert Bender (11)*
*King Henry VIII School*

## THE SILVER STALLION

A silver stallion stands, alert.
Watching proudly over mares and foals.
He rears up,
Arched neck,
Mane and tail cascading down.

A silver ghost,
Enticing mares to play.
The snow starts
Drifting silently down,
Befriending him.

The stallion rolls,
Stands up, shakes,
Snow flies off him.
A soft powder falling
From an icing sugar statue.

*Ellie Davis (10)*
*King Henry VIII School*

## IN THE BIN

You always wonder what's in the bin,
A winning scratch card could be in,
Cans and bottles,
Fruit and veg,
Smelly socks and a wooden ledge.

You always wonder what's in the bin,
Some rotten old books and a fish's fin,
Sweet papers,
Dirty rags,
A pencil case and big black bags.

You always wonder what's in the bin,
A cardboard box and a baked bean tin,
A fish's head,
A fox' tail,
A snail shell and yesterday's mail.

***Mark Edwards  (11)***
***King Henry VIII School***


## I'M GONNA LIVE FOREVER

Sit at my window,
And dream of what could be,
Maybe what should be,
Happening to me.

'My life: The movie'
The script would cover reams.
Life through a lens,
Or so it seems.

Creased magazines,
Reminders of the past.
A programme from *Fame*
I was in the cast.

Still, what's gone is gone,
You can't turn back time.
But what use are clichés?
And is wishing a crime?

*Octavia Younger (12)*
*King Henry VIII School*


## ADULTS

Adults are always shouting and getting really cross.
But then I opened my mouth
And showed them who was boss.
But they said they were in charge
And they said they'd hit me if I shouted at them again.
But I said, 'Well you shouldn't always get cross then.'
And my mum said, 'Get back here this instant,
I'm warning you young lady.'
But I just ignored her and met up with my friend Brady.
We went to the park and had some fun,
And played around in the shining sun.
When the night was over, I went home to my parents
And said that I was sorry and I'd never do that again.

*Keriane Garton (13)*
*King Henry VIII School*

## MY GRANDMA!

My grandma has a motor bike,
A Norton Sixty Five.
She mends it in the garage,
And does wheelies in the drive.

She speeds along the country lanes,
She terrorises sheep.
She's made a jump, from a rotten plank,
Propped against a manure heap!

She's been all over England,
She's wanted far and wide,
For driving on the motorway,
The wrong way and wrong side!

My grandma's thinking of giving it up.
The motor bike I mean.
She wants to race at Ascot,
On a horse called Butter Bean!

*Imogen Hassall  (13)*
*King Henry VIII School*


## RATS, RATS, RATS

Rats, rats, rats doing what they please
Scratching on the kitchen floor and
Eating up the cheese.
Hiding in the basement,
Hiding in your shoe,
Get the double barrel and blow them all to
                    *Goo!*

*Simon Jones  (12)*
*King Henry VIII School*

104

## SHADOWS

When the sun comes out,
The shadows come out to play,
Tall shadows and short shadows,
Dancing shadows and still shadows,
Prancing shadows and darting shadows,
They are all made by the sun,
The shadows come out to play all day,
They play games and have fun all day,
Then suddenly the sun goes down,
Rapidly shadows are fading,
Slipping neatly away,
Put away for another day,
Then at the same time,
The very next day,
The shadows again come out to play.

*Anthony Chaloner (11)*
*King Henry VIII School*

## HALLOWE'EN

H allowe'en
A ngry blood-thirsty creations drool
L ingering in the corner, eyes wide with hunger
L ong uneven teeth bathe in a pool of saliva
O n old Hallows Eve the dead are awakened
W itches comb the night air
E ntrances of abodes protected by an
E nchanted lantern
N o soul dare venture the beyond.

*Joe Atkinson (11)*
*King Henry VIII School*

## SID, FROM THE SUN

My desk's at the back of the class
And nobody, nobody knows
I'm Sid from the sun.
With a red, fiery body and a light bulb for a nose,
I have green ears and hair which is soft as gold.
I have no teeth, no fingers, no toes.
My head is a ball of sapphire blue.
My eyes are green and I look very mean but
Nobody, nobody knows.
They would scream with fear when there was
Nobody near.
They would trash the toys.
Pull their fingers down the board,
And crawl on the floor.
Then I will stand up and walk out of the door.

*Sam Tutton  (11)*
*King Henry VIII School*


## HALLOWE'EN

H  allowe'en is very scary
A  rachnophobers big and hairy
L  iving in a horrid house is very scary
L  ooking round for lots of sweets
O  h no, here's a spider
W  itches are cooking stew
E  ating lots of people
E  ven though they are not tasty
N  othing is scarier than Hallowe'en.

*Daniel Matthews  (11)*
*King Henry VIII School*

## MEMORIES

Memories of when the sun rose
and the wind blew a gentle breeze,
and the buttercups turned around to stare at
the cows waking.
The early morning dew lifts from its comfy
resting place.

Memories of when the snow lay
on the glistening mountains.
The robin sang on the naked branch
of a willow tree.

Memories of when the buds burst out
into the warmth of the sun.
The smell of new life
filled the air with a smile.
Memories.

*Sally Brinkworth  (13)*
*King Henry VIII School*


## NAT

I have a girlfriend called Nat
I love her to bits, that's a fact
Her eyes sparkle like sunlight
Her hair shines like the sun.
She's the most beautiful girl in the world,
I love her to bits, that's a fact.

*Alex Linney  (12)*
*King Henry VIII School*

## ON SUCH A NIGHT

The mountain seems to rumble,
Trees look like giant hunchbacks,
Owls hoot and bats squeal
Houses stand out against the moonlight,
On such a night.

Are there shapes lurking in the distance?
Do they move ever so slowly?
Are they threatening to attack me?
Will they reach me here? I hope not!
On such a night!

No matter!
I'm safe in my lovely warm house.
With no teddy bear by my side.
No, they can't reach me here, can they?
On such a night!

*Lloyd Hughes (12)*
*King Henry VIII School*

## THE VAMPIRE

It swooshes and flaps as a bat
With a flash, a bang and a roar
He lands there on the floor . . . *Thump!*
Its unfortunate victim bellows
The vampire shouts 'Hello'
With a beam of sunlight
The vampire screams as he frazzles and sizzles.

*Jamie Breakwell (11)*
*King Henry VIII School*

## ANIMALS IN DANGER

Tigers, elephants and gorillas
are all animals in danger.
Shooting, stabbing, torturing
being killed every minute, every day.

Dolphins, seals and sealions
are all sea animals in danger.
Shooting, catching, eating
being eaten every second of the day.

It's so cruel
It's not right
They didn't do anything to you!

*Claire Addis  (12)*
*King Henry VIII School*


## THE BALLERINA

Twirling softly on her points
Gracefully arching her arms
Glittering in her sparkly dress
The audience, bewitched by her charms
As she pirouettes across the stage
The conductor quickly turns his page
The soothing rhythms of the music flow
The twinkling white lights dazzle like snow
As the green velvet curtains finally close
The dancer is given a single red rose.

*Catherine Lock  (11)*
*King Henry VIII School*

## WATCH OUT!

Watch out!
There's a big, brown bear outside your door,
Watch out!
There's a big, brown and green gorilla in your bed,
Watch out!
There's a smelly, pongy skunk in the bath,
Watch out!
There's a blood-sucking vampire bat in your shoe,
Watch out!
There's a frightening monster behind your door, waiting to say *Boo!*

*Rebekah Anne Brown (11)*
*King Henry VIII School*


## HALLOWE'EN

H ubble, toil and trouble
A arrh! Shriek, cry the children
L aughing, cackle, cry the witches
L ow swooping, more witches fly by
O ver a distance this noise is heard
W ailing as the children are eaten
E very Hallowe'en the ghost appears
E verlasting, creepy sound
N ever before have I seen such a terror.

*Heather Venfield (11)*
*King Henry VIII School*

## HONESTY

If a promise you don't keep
It will haunt you in your sleep
And as you lie beneath your quilt
You will have a conscience full of guilt

If a secret you do tell
You will not feel very well
It will go round your brain
Until your head is full of pain.

If a lie you do make
You will be seen as a fake
Alone you will always be
And no friends you will see.

Keep a promise, don't tell a lie
Keep secrets, no need to cry
Your life will be good and true
And people will believe in you.

*Harriet Artes (11)*
*King Henry VIII School*

## RUGBY

R ugby is a man's game
U nder the bar miss.
G reat try by the forward.
B all flying over the bar! Great conversion.
Y esterday Wales beat England 33-20.

*Sam Morgan (12)*
*King Henry VIII School*

## RAILWAY LINE

Rushing down the railway,
Steaming down the track,
The next stop's not far away,
The last is miles back,
The whistle blows,
We're doing fine,
Steaming down this railway line.
Stopping at the stations,
Letting people out,
'Our train is here,'
The people would shout,
The green flag waves,
Let's make up lost time,
Puffing down this railway line.

*James Clement  (12)*
*King Henry VIII School*


## HALLOWE'EN

H  oot, howl, hubble bubble,
A  rgh, toil and trouble,
L  egs of frogs, eyes of spiders,
L  et's heat a cauldron, and make potions . . .
O  r we'll catch children!
W  e shall marinade them in gooey . . .
E  gg sauce and salt and pepper.
'E  lp! cry the children, we'll be witches' soup.
N  ow then children! Cackle the witches,
     are you ready to be 'gloop'?

*Hannah Shaw  (11)*
*King Henry VIII School*

## LOVE POEM

My love for thee is deeper than the
deepest dark blue sea,
No matter how far away thou art
I will always think of thee.
I think of thee all day and night
even when thou art out of sight.

Of the roses in the summer time
and the walks around the park,
The night thou lost thy torch and I
chased thee in the dark.
Thine eyes are brown, thy hair is
blond,
It wasn't half funny when thou
fell in the pond.

*Robbie Baines  (11)*
*King Henry VIII School*

## FOOTBALL

F  ootball is the best
O  *ffside* said the ref
O  ne-nil to Man Utd
T  wo-nil, Cole just scored
B  ad time for Liverpool
A  fter the match, I get drunk
L  iverpool
L  ost.

*Shaun Robinson  (12)*
*King Henry VIII School*

## DOGS

Dogs are all sorts,
Black, white and brown.
There are loads of types of dogs,
Spaniels, terriers and hounds.

Dogs come in all different sizes,
Large, medium and small.
Dogs can also be
Short or tall.

Dogs can be
Cuddly, cute and fluffy,
Or they can be
Fierce, vicious and naughty.

*Sarah Phillips  (11)*
*King Henry VIII School*

## UFOs

What's that in the distance?
A great, bright light
I got out of the car
But it zoomed out of sight
I paused for a moment
What could it be?
Was it for real?
Or too much TV?
Could it be I just don't know
I think it was a UFO.

*Jonathan Hill  (12)*
*King Henry VIII School*

## THERE'S A MONSTER UNDER MY BED!

There's a monster under my bed,
that looks really scary.
He's got bright, glowing, red eyes,
and he's all wrinkly and hairy.

I went to bed last night,
started watching the telly.
His head started to appear,
and then I saw his belly!

I screamed my head off loudly,
the monster went bright blue.
I though he'd disappeared,
but then I heard a *boo!*

*Katie Stokes (11)*
*King Henry VIII School*


## EVERYONE GO PARTY

Boys and girls in the dance hall,
All in their disco outfits,
Girls are in their make-up and glitter in their hair,
Boys looking cool with gelled hair,
Music thumping,
Lights flashing,
Boys and girls start dancing to the slow song,
Eating and drinking and having fun.

*Stephanie Harvey-Meates (13)*
*King Henry VIII School*

## Romeo and Juliet

Romeo and Juliet,
Oh, what a play.
Romeo and Juliet,
They have a lot to say.

Shakespeare, Shakespeare,
He's such a dramatist.
Romance and love,
Sent by a dove.

Hatred and death,
Swords clash and clang.
Hope and despair
Sent by a crow.

The strongest friendship,
Full of hope and love.
No one can part them,
Romeo and Juliet.

*Stephanie Davies  (11)*
*King Henry VIII School*


## The River

Splashing, flowing, dripping, swishing,
Racing down the mountain.
Carrying leaves, twigs, bits and bobs.
Unfortunate insects getting washed away.
Finally the river reaches the sea.
Free to move around, through the salty water.

*Matthew Clark  (12)*
*King Henry VIII School*

## BABY, BABY, BABY

Smelly nappies,
cry, cry, cry,
and wakes me up in the night,
please shut up.
I take my homework to the teacher,
and in my horror, baby drool,
I tell my teacher but
'Oh not excuses, excuses'
that's what she said,
and put me straight to detention.
I go home tired and went straight to bed,
Ah,
babies, who wants them?
Definitely not me!

*Daniel Harris  (11)*
*King Henry VIII School*




## THE WEATHER

On a sunny day there's lots of time to play,
When it's windy and bright I can fly my kite,
When it's cold, snowy and sad, there's sledging fun to be had,
When it's pouring with rain there's mud and it's a dreadful pain,
When it's cold there's a hot water bottle to hold,
Sometimes when it's boring and cool you even want to go to *school!*

*Richard Alldred  (12)*
*King Henry VIII School*

## DIANA

She will never again be seen,
Or never again be heard
But Diana our faithful queen,
The queen of hearts,
The queen of joy,
The queen of happiness,
To every girl and boy.

We will love you till the end of time,
And forever more,
For Diana our faithful queen,
Our queen of hearts,
Our queen of joy,
Our queen of happiness,
We love you so.

William and Harry are luckiest of all
To have had a mother who cared for all.
Who cared for the poor,
Who cared for the sick,
With her eyes which
Could melt people's hearts with their twinkle,
And her smile that warmed everyone up.
We know all this because it simply did happen . . .
To each and every one of us!

*Louise Pryse-Evans  (12)*
*King Henry VIII School*

## THE CANDLE

Darkness, emptiness, nothingness.
Then light.
A match strikes, a candle is lit.
Gentle flickering bathes the room with its glimmer,
Its illuminating rays, filling all the corners.
The wax droplets bleed from the candle's light.
Down to the base where they set.
A window slides open,
A gentle breath puts the light to sleep.
Darkness, emptiness, nothingness.

*Andrew Knight (13)*
*King Henry VIII School*


## MY DAD WANTS TO BE A TREE

My dad wants to be a tree
But I won't let him be
For the havoc he may cause
The world will surely pause
To see this sight
That's sure to bring delight
Especially on Bonfire Night.

*Jennifer Cheesman (12)*
*King Henry VIII School*

## THE OWL

The owl comes out late at night,
If you should be lucky to see him, he's a beautiful sight.
Big eyes staring,
Big eyes glaring,
He really can give you a fright,
This beautiful bird of the night,
Mr Owl flying free
I wish I was you,
And you were me,
But then you eat mice for tea,
So I'm glad I'm me.

*Matthew Llewellyn  (11)*
*King Henry VIII School*


## FOOTBALL

F  ootball is a great game,
O  f skill and fun,
O  ne-nil said the supporters,
T  wo-nil said the ref,
B  attled out to be the cup holders,
A  nd to be the best team,
L  iverpool can't get a goal,
L  iverpool lost.

*Scott Owen  (12)*
*King Henry VIII School*

## THE LOVERS

I'm on the beach
watching the tide come in.
Something catches the corner
of my eye.

There were lovers
looking eye to eye.
Holding hands and kissing.

Someday I'll be in love,
Someday I'll be like those.
But someday hasn't come
yet for me.

*Carmelle Timothy  (12)*
*King Henry VIII School*


## A DAY FISHING

Sitting on a riverbank
Rain, wind or shine
Putting worms and maggots
Onto hook and line
Watch the float bob and sway
Waiting for a bite
Strike, pull, reel it in
The fish puts up a fight.

*Luke Shaw  (12)*
*King Henry VIII School*

## GUESS WHAT?

Brown, white or black,
With a tail on its back,
Four legs it has.

Spots, patches or plain,
With a long or short mane,
Has a saddle on its back.

Grass, hay or maize
In its stable it likes to laze
Large teeth it has.

*Guess what*
*?*

*esroh a*

**Stacey Harris  (12)**
**King Henry VIII School**


## SNAKES

Some snakes have rattles on their tails,
Poison they spit as they dance,
Slithering, sliding and hiding,
As it gets ready to pounce on its prey,
Quick as the speed of sound,
But silent, no sound it makes,
Then it pounces, kills its prey instantly,
Beautiful but deadly,
And so elegant.

**Stacey Stevens  (11)**
**King Henry VIII School**

## GINGER AND WHITE

Ginger and white,
with whiskers too,
a long striped tail,
with four stumpy paws,
big, brown eyes, wide and round,
prances up and down the garden path,
jumping over stepping stones,
bouncing up and down.
This is my kitten *Domino.*

Catches butterflies and chases leaves,
as they come swirling and twirling down,
plays with string, tennis balls and skipping ropes,
hurtles over the grass, tail following proudly.

*Amanda Thomas  (12)*
*King Henry VIII School*


## WHAT IS?

What is white? A swan is white, sailing in the light.
What is pink? A flamingo is pink, as tall as you and I.
What is yellow? A chick is yellow, newly born today.
What is blue? A dolphin is blue, dancing on the waves.
What is green? A grass snake is green, slithering over the land.
What is grey? An elephant is grey, walking in a herd.
What is black? A panther is black, stalking its prey.

*Sarah Briggs  (11)*
*King Henry VIII School*

# FEAR

Shaking, shivering, shifting shadows,
the floorboards creak;
The mouse breaks the silence with a squeak.
A spider crawls, then falls,
cobwebs hang still upon the walls.

Nowhere to go, the fear starts to flow
as wicked winds begin to blow.
I pull the covers over my head
through all the fear my father said,
'Son, you are safe inside your bed.'

The room is hot
but I am not
Too scared to look
I throw a book.

In that corner I see a shape,
a wicked man who wears a cape.
His face is wrinkly and long,
he looks grey and very strong.

The man floats like Peter Pan
he hops and skips around my room
In fear I throw a wooden spoon
he turns around and comes to ground

'Hey, boy,' he says 'do you know who I am?
For I am not Peter Pan. I am old yet I am young
you can never ever run
*For I am fear!'*

***Ben Burns (14)***
***King Henry VIII School***

## VOLCANO

One moment a silent mountain,
The next all fire bared.
One moment all is peaceful,
But then a war is declared!

Hot, thick, red liquid,
Shoot from a gap full of might.
It then flows across the once fresh land,
Destroying all in its sight.

Creating a dark, new surface,
As it oozes from deep beneath,
Leaving its path of destruction,
With sharp, cutting rocks like teeth.

All you can do is prepare,
For the time when it will strike again.
To prevent all suffering and damage,
And to rule out all hurt and all pain.

*Kate Allison  (14)*
*King Henry VIII School*


## PETS

My Nan has a dog called Sonny.
Some of the things that
he does seem funny.
When chasing a ball he goes
into a roll, turns over
and lands on his tummy.

*Lydia Frost  (11)*
*King Henry VIII School*

## TRUE LOVE OR NOT?

You see him as yours,
His lips!
His eyes!
Heaven?
What more could you want?
You think this is it,
He loves you!
You love him!
Heaven?
What more could you want?
But be careful!
Cinderella?
Snow White?
Is all this for real?
Is this what you want?

*Penny Knight (12)*
*King Henry VIII School*


## FOR LOVE OF THE SKY

Whooshing through the clouds,
Through the clear blue air,
High above land,
The plane soars through the sky,
Out above the ocean,
Watching boats sail by,
Oh I love the sky,
The sky so high.

*Rachael Louise Knight (11)*
*King Henry VIII School*

## NOTHING

I'm confused, stars, lights!
Nothing is right, moon, sun!
Pain and torture are of the heart.
I hate life, I'd rather happiness,
Love is pain, time is worthless.
Nothing is nought,
Nought is nothing.
Time in life means nothing to me,
I'm thinking things.
Universe planets.
The atmosphere is a wonderful place
I watch, I watch,
Prison, home
Horrid, warm cheeks.
All in life means nothing, my life
Come stars, come night
Come out to play.
Planets, planets in the sky,
Where do they come from?
My oh my,
Here comes day, me and
The planets only just got to play.
Bye bye night, oh precious love,
Time is wasted on day
I love the night, what's your
Favourite time?
Love oh love for the sky!

*Zoë Harney  (11)*
*King Henry VIII School*

## GOING TO MARKET

I like going to market.
On an early Friday morning.
I slip on my wellies and my red overalls.
The sky covered in fog and glistening dew.
The cattle are in the orchard, Kap our
sheepdog rounds them up.
We load two blonde charalais,
We're off to Ross Market.
The hustle and bustle of talking farmers.
Cows are bawling and the yearlings baaring.
Hot teas are being sold.
A man sounds the bell for the cattle
The auctioneer crying out for bids
We travel home tired.

*Jamie Edwards  (13)*
*King Henry VIII School*

## CHRISTMAS TIME

Christmas is fun,
Christmas is jolly,
with all its mistletoe
and all its holly.
Presents galore,
all children shout 'More!'
The goose is getting fat,
because it's to be eaten and that's *that!*

*Michelle Jones  (11)*
*King Henry VIII School*

## HALLOWE'EN

The witches fly past the moon,
with long drifting black cloaks,
the slight breeze that blows through the dark.
The ghosts that *scream*,
in the darkness big black eyes in the moonlight.
Little children
running screaming
trick or treating.
Lots of yummy sweets piled up in pockets,
some hidden under their hats.

The black cats stroll,
pumpkins lit up in the windows,
children laugh in the background.
Witches cackle and giggle and go back to their cave
back to sleep for another year.
Children run home to bed,
eating their sweets as the clock strikes midnight.
Hallowe'en is nearly over.

*Michelle Hancock (12)*
*King Henry VIII School*


## MY BROTHER

I have a brother, he lives in his room,
When he comes downstairs, off I go, *zoom!*
He really is noisy, he really is a pain,
When I turn the telly on, he turns it off again.
He buys me sweets when he's in the mood,
But he takes them off me again, if I don't eat my food.

*Bethan Vaughan (12)*
*King Henry VIII School*

## I SHOULD LIKE TO PAINT

I should like to paint
the wind travelling through the trees.

I should like to paint
the sound of a snake hissing as it catches its prey.

I should like to paint
the sound of our voices chattering and whispering.

I should like to paint
the sound of the flutter of wings.

And last, I should like to paint
the quiet gossip of insects scurrying to and fro.

*Jennifer Fry (11)*
*King Henry VIII School*


## ALEX'S HAIR

Tall, straight, sticky
Sometimes covered in wax
Short, black, itchy
Never combed back.
A centre of attention
That makes people stare
A tall, black wave
Of combed, gelled hair.

*Jack Watkins (11)*
*King Henry VIII School*

## THE BOTTOM OF THE BED!

I lie awake,
It's midnight,
The clock chimes,
Where am I?

Hello . . . hello
Is someone there?
I look, I stare
But still no one's there!

I hear a noise,
Bang, thud, bang,
Who is it?
What is it?

*Lianne Trickey  (12)*
*King Henry VIII School*


## OUR MONSTER TEACHER

We have a monster teacher, she's yellow, black and blue,
you never want to go near her, just in case she's got the flu.
Her teeth are brown, her nails are long,
she's very weird so she must have been born wrong.
None of us like the old bat,
because they think she's a witch, because she's got a black cat.
At lunchtime she's always hanging around a big tree,
I think she's there because she's lost her lucky key.
At the end of the day I'm glad to go,
because she says 'No, no, you're not allowed to go.'

*Charlotte Cooke  (12)*
*King Henry VIII School*

# PAIN

My life is seen through the eyes of a lonely old man,
The knowledge of the islands lie deep within my heart,
Those wizened, rickety old legs that tread those many steps,
Secret so special and important and deep,
Raging to burst from out of my body,
Friendship I desire a friend indeed,
A name The Birdman?
Do they know how strong it may hurt?
Damage deep,
Listen to the cry,
My life is animals.

*Sarah Holden (12)*
*King Henry VIII School*

# SHARKS

The great white shark, a killer fiend, a blood-thirsty bandit
to make you scream.
But have you seen his gentle side, a swift silhouette on the
sea-bed sands, a slinky creature who looks quite grand.
With a snap of his jaws it will bite you in half.
A swift tail swishes from side to side,
Among the seaweed it does hide
with a band of killers by its side.

*Sarah Diamond (11)*
*King Henry VIII School*

## THE PANDA

On first impressions:
The panda so cute and cuddly,
Spending hours eating,
Happy with himself as company,
Waddling peacefully from place to place,
His thick fur giving him protection in winter,
Safe, surrounded by bamboo.

But . . .
He's under threat!
People destroy his food,
They just don't care.
A solitary animal, humans disregard him,
Tossed aside like school books.
No chance to stand up for himself!

If only people thought of him as I do.

*Richard Sutton  (12)*
*King Henry VIII School*


## MY BAD AIM

Footy is my favourite game
Worst of all is my bad aim
Up and over, long and wide
Still I manage to keep my pride
Never right, always wrong
My foot is like a big ding-dong
I give my all when I hit the ball
But still it will not hit the goal.

*Nathan Jarrold  (12)*
*King Henry VIII School*

## THE CASTLE OF HORROR

He stepped towards the huge, dark shadow,
And felt a shiver run down his spine,
He heard a scream,
He knew it wasn't a dream,
He knew that it was for real.

The huge oak gates flew open,
He heard a gust of wind,
The darkness got even darker,
And a deep voice called him in.

He climbed up the spiral stairway,
A clatter was heard behind,
He reached the top, and there he stopped,
The witch there was so unkind.

The witch was stirring up her brew,
And then back down the steps, the man flew,
A figure was standing in the man's way,
But the man didn't stop, and the figure paid.

The man ran up to the castle wall,
And over it he climbed,
But when he got up to the top,
I won't mention what he'll find!

*Adam Peacock  (12)*
*King Henry VIII School*

## DOGS

Dogs in the garden,
dogs are in the living room,
dogs in the garbage.

My dog is fierce,
my dog is also crazy,
always barking mad.

She plays all night,
fights all day with cats and dogs,
tiny and playful.

I don't care if you,
Mum, don't like my dog Lucky,
who barks very loudly.

*Samantha Smith (11)*
*King Henry VIII School*


## TITANIC

It sailed across the ocean sea,
It sailed to the land of the free,
The boat was sturdy it would float,
Oh how they all did gloat,
Until it struck a piece of ice,
Which probably wasn't very nice,
People ran around and cried,
But oh so many of them died,
The boat was sinking,
The water it was drinking,
The people in the water froze,
And then their eyes began to close,
Then the water swallowed the Titanic,
Down it went without a panic,
Now it lies at the bottom of the sea,
What a sight I'd like to see.

*James Williams (12)*
*King Henry VIII School*

## CHILD

A butterfly spreads its wings
Over a child's heart,
Blocking it from warmth,
A cold heart,
A sad child
Hangs
Like a picture on the wall,
The life of a child seems happy to me,
Yet this sad, inanimate child is
Lifeless and blue,
Starved from breath.
Let the child live.
Show it warmth, and life,
Show it how to
Live.

*Lydia Morgan  (12)*
*King Henry VIII School*

## LIGHT

L  apping up the land with wondrous rays.
I  magining the world without it.
G  loomy and dark without life or days.
H  ints of a shadow where light isn't lit.
T  he light of the sun is warm and don't spoil it!

*Laura Roberts  (12)*
*King Henry VIII School*

## MY GARDEN

Springtime flowers in yellow and gold,
Time for the new to replace the old.
Tulips and daffodils start to flower,
Nodding their heads in an April shower.

Summer sun is here at last,
Bringing flowers thick and fast.
Some in pink, some in cream,
All the colours you could dream.

Colourful leaves start to fall,
Beginning to build a frosty wall.
Shiny conkers drop to the floor,
All the flowers are dead and poor.

As the flowers prepare to sleep,
They bow their heads as if to weep.
All that is left is the wintry sun,
To light up my garden now that its work is done.

*Katy Pritchard  (11)*
*King Henry VIII School*


## THE ISLES OF SCILLY

Peaceful and calm paradise,
Warm and sunny paradise,
White beaches in my paradise,
Blue seas in my paradise,
The isles of Scilly is my paradise.

*Jonathan Like  (12)*
*King Henry VIII School*

## THE HAUNTED HOUSE

I went into the house,
It was dark and frightening.
I looked outside it was thundering and lightning.
All the bones in my body were shaking,
I whispered aloud, my voice was quaking.

I walked up the first stair,
Should I go any further?
I looked around, I heard a noise,
I blinked and turned,
Nothing was there.
My imagination was running wild
What should I do?
I ran to the door.

*Laura Maddrell  (12)*
*King Henry VIII School*


## THE WOOD

I went into the wood one day,
and as I walked I lost my way,
when it was too dark to see,
a little creature came up to me,
he said if I would come along,
he would sing me a happy song,
we walked along I held it tight,
because the wood gave me a fright,
he sang a song and let me go,
he went away the wind started to blow.

*Jason Curtis  (12)*
*King Henry VIII School*

# KILLING A FOX

As the hunter gets on the horse
and rides away,
The dogs are loose and are on their way
to find some prey,
They smell it a mile away
hopping one, two, three hedges
along the way.
He has him in his sight
'Bang',
blood all over, the fox is dead,
the hounds are fed.

*Scott Elmore  (12)*
*King Henry VIII School*

# WINTER

Winter warm, winter cold,
Winter is cold and dull,
Yet houses in winter are warm and cosy,
With soup brewing and the fire burning.
Outside the snow is falling,
The icy cold keeping everything indoors.
Winter warm, winter cold,
Will winter go?
Will winter stay another day?

*Siân Harrington  (12)*
*King Henry VIII School*

## FRIENDS!

Friends are people you can trust,
and never ever say you must.
They are good fun and a big laugh,
and help you to clean out your bath.
They are either a girl or boy,
and occasionally will lend a toy.
I have friends all over the world,
and some of them, their hair is curled.
You talk to them about your problems,
and give them a should for a sob.
You help them with their families' needs,
and feel good after doing a good deed.
You give them a hug,
send them home with a bug,
that you caught off a friend,
and now it's the end.

*Samantha Harris  (11)*
*King Henry VIII School*

## THE DOLPHIN

In the South Atlantic ocean,
Lives a dolphin with its young,
Flying through the water like a bird in the air,
Diving to the bottom and coming back for air,
Spiralling and looping like an acrobat on land,
As fast as a beach buggy travelling along the sand.

*Sam Vaughan  (12)*
*King Henry VIII School*

## A GIRLY POEM

On no, she's broken a nail,
her hair is in a mess,
she wants to go home,
she likes making a fuss.

She has really good manners,
she says please and thank you,
she is tidy and neat,
she is very organised.

They hate housework,
such as ironing, hoovering,
some love cooking a lot,
some can't cook.

They play sport,
they ride their horses,
they play lacrosse,
they hate rugby and other contact sports.

She's very fast, and very nimble,
she has good ball control,
she loves rugby,
she doesn't mind getting wet and dirty.

She's my mum,
she's my sister,
they're my friends,
one day she may be my daughter.

*Thomas Picton-Turbervill (13)*
*Monmouth School*

## GREAT AND GRUESOME GIRLS

There are different types of girls,
A girl which is like a girl,
And a girl which is like a boy,
Girls which are rude or polite,
Girls which are pretty or ugly,
Here I would like to explain.

This one is pretty,
And she is also sporty,
Intelligent too,
And she is kind,
And popular,
Surprise! She is a girl.

This one is ugly,
And also unsporty,
Unintelligent too,
In school no one likes her,
She is not popular,
Surprise! She is a girl.

There are different types,
They are not all polite,
Always through puberty,
They will sometimes have chores,
Female products - and more!
But listen - they are girls.

You can fall in love with one,
Or despise one,
Eventually babies,
Marriage too,
But in the teens come dating,
They are our girls.

*Alexander Rushworth (13)*
*Monmouth School*

## ASK ME AGAIN WHEN I'M 21!

All they do is fuss,
Wondering at their hair,
Asking about their nails,
Commenting on their make-up.
It's never-ending,
Annoying,
Boring,
Everlasting!

Though they can be a good laugh,
Smell sweetly
And have kind hearts.
They are tremendous fun
And they can be a friend.
They're great at listening
And pretending to understand,
Though I'll never understand them!

So, are they boring,
Annoying,
Fussy?
Well ask me again,
When I'm 21!

*James Widnall (13)*
*Monmouth School*

## GIRLS ARE DIFFERENT

There are lots of different types of girls,
Some are short, some are tall,
Some are fat, some are thin.
Some like boys, some do not.
Some like sports, others do not.
Some worry about what they wear, some do not.

One thing that is sure is that not all girls are the same.
In fact no girl is identical.
No girl is the same.
That's what makes them so different.

Of course they have things in common.
They are all around us.
Some watching our every move.
If they look different,
They often have inner things in common.
*What is this?*

***James Richards (13)***
***Monmouth School***

## CONTRAST

Aeroplanes and dolls,
Footballs and horses.
Mountain biking and skipping,
Boys and girls.

Hard and soft,
Strong and weak.
Aggressive and sensitive,
Boys and girls.

Interesting and boring,
Organised and chaotic.
Careerist and lazy,
Girls and boys.

*Jethro Binns  (14)*
*Monmouth School*


## FIRST IMPRESSIONS

Girls are an alien species,
Who walk our Earth and live among us,
They infiltrate our homes and schools
And make a misery of our lives.

They inhabit not human bodies,
But ones with lumps in all the wrong places,
They congregate in groups and chatter
In their squeaking, high-pitched language.

Their only pastime is a sort of game,
Throwing an orange sphere into a hoop,
They don their battle-clothes, bearing a code,
GK, GA, C, what can this all mean?

Girls are incapable of communicating
With any *normal* species,
Talking is useless; they just look puzzled,
Then run away to find a fellow alien.

What happens to them at nights?
I have never seen one outside of school,
Yet some poor souls have them in their homes,
Then they bear an alias - 'sisters'!

*James Bridges  (14)*
*Monmouth School*

## GIRLS ARE ALL THE SAME

Alice bands and curly hair,
Ginger, dark or maybe fair,
Girls are all the same.

They borrow your things,
And mess them up,
They like angels wings,
And fairy things,
Girls are all the same.

Grown up now,
With fashion toes,
Music blaring,
And boyfriends staring,
Wardrobe growing,
And lava-lamp glowing.

Girls are all the same!

*Rhys Thomson  (13)*
*Monmouth School*


## BOYS ON GIRLS

Women are women and men are men,
But pity me please for I am only ten,
They look so different they look so strange,
I think I'll keep well out of range.

They plait their hair,
They bat their eyes,
They do things men just despise,
But they don't really mind.

Men just sit and stare at them for hours,
Or gel their hair and give them flowers.
And so I don't think I will be able to
Tell how they work or what they do.

*William Jacks (14)*
*Monmouth School*


## SEXIST VIEW

Boys on girls,
Can be appealing,
To girls, who knows?
But they can be shocked,
At what we think,
And make them despise us even more,
Our hearts will break,
Our eyes will cry,
And we would wish that we would die.

Girls,
What are they like?
Having manicures, body massages,
Which costs a bomb!
And when they are lonely or sad,
They cry and have temper tantrums,
In the midst of the day.

But on the bright side . . .
They have great assets,
And they also have great conversational skills,
Which we tend to lack,
But overall we are better,
Than sensitive, gentle, fragile girls.

*Andrew Woo (14)*
*Monmouth School*

## A - Z OF GIRLS

Anorexic models,
Broken nails,
Conditioners and shampoos,
Dark secrets,
Exotic clothes,
Fashion mags,
Girls' day out,
Hair problems,
Irresistable boys,
Juvenile people,
Knickers,
Leo di Caprio,
Mini skirts,
Nail varnish,
Oxyten,
Period pains,
Romantic movies,
Shopping sprees,
Tampons,
Uniform,
Viagra,
What to wear,
X-Files
Yelling tantrums,
Zits.

Not to mention all the dieting, the manicuring, the . . . etc!

*Steven Nowosad  (13)*
*Monmouth School*

## MY BROTHER

My brother is a show-off,
Always trying to impress.
He always wants attention,
He wants lots of girls around him.
Refuses to wear last year's fashion in case
　　　　　　　　　　　his friends see him.
He'll then be unpopular
Which just won't do.

My brother thinks he's tough,
But really he's a coward.
He picks on people younger than him
But never anyone his own size.
He's football mad,
He'll play al day.
When I ask to join in he says,
'Don't be silly it's a man's sport, go away.'

All boys are like this,
Try to impress, but they don't one bit.
But there are some special boys
Who are sweet and cute.
I haven't yet come across one
As there are very few of them.

*Matt Legg  (14)*
*Monmouth School*

## SEXY!

G ruesome people of the earth,
I diots and careless from birth!
R ampaging pieces of lard,
L ets burn them make them charred!
S ucking on fags on the street,

O nly girls are sometimes sweet!
N o use to the world,

B oys could be nice, oh yes they could!
O nly one half of our race,
Y ou may be one, what a disgrace!
S ometimes friendly, what a joke!

*Ben Gaulton (13)*
*Monmouth School*


## BOYS ON GIRLS

Will we ever understand the female race?
The constant battle of feminine and masculine rights
This boundary of difference

This division that men fail to cross
This line that forms the curiosity of gender
This equator that fuels our relationships

This god-placed boundary
These differences that separate us, join us.

*Sam Small (13)*
*Monmouth School*

## GIRL TALK

In my grand experience there are three types of girls,
Their brands being Tom Girl, Forward Girl and Cutie Girl.
All these are deadly in their own right,
i.e. - don't pick a fight!

Forward Girl's tactics are heavy make-up and perfume,
Avoid her like the plague, she could wipe out a platoon,
Also beware of bleached hair,
Avoid it if you can as well as fake tan.

Cutie Girl's tactics are all innocent and cute,
Dodge them if you can for it's enough to make you puke!
Simpering on the corner, she'll avoid your eye,
Steer clear for you're bound to make her cry.

Tom Girl's tactics are hanging with your mates,
Sly comments like, 'Nice girlfriend,' can determine your fate,
Also watch out for mega-short hair,
Bypass her if you can (but this type is very rare).

*James Green  (13)*
*Monmouth School*